Dear Target reader (or shall we say *Targét* reader),

We are truly honored to have the opportunity to share this book, our labor of love, with you, as well as offer special behind-the-scenes details of the making of *Yes Way Rosé: A Guide to the Pink Wine State of Mind.*

When we set out to write our first book, there was so much we wanted to accomplish. We wanted to tell the story of how we went from friends to owners of a wine and lifestyle brand, with dreams of inspiring readers. We wanted to establish our authorité on the subject of rosé. We wanted to offer a fun and user-friendly resource on the winemaking process, flavor profiles, and where rosé is produced across the globe, revealing why our favorite wine is so delectable. We wanted to provide endless ways to enjoy the pink drink with our favorite food pairings, cocktail recipes, and entertaining tips. And most importantly, we wanted to deliver it all with a sense of humor. Our lighthearted tone is intended to reflect the spirit of this beautiful pink wine. We think it's pretty hysterical that a beverage is so pleasing and has made such a difference in our lives—it's why we are obsessed with it!

We are best friends *and* business partners, and everything we do as YWR is a true collaboration. We began the book process by going through years of our @yeswayrose Instagram feed, first launched in 2013, to get in the zone. This trip down memory lane led to the idea for recreating our best posts and puns, which you will find on page 100. The writing was a constant back and forth, with countless drafts. Working on this project wasn't always easy, but when you're trying to make your friend laugh, there's a level of satisfaction when you finallé do. We proofread the pages over and over, with at least five rounds focused just on our use of the iconic aigu accent for consistencé.

The highlight of the process was working with our creative team on capturing the photos you'll see throughout the book. We shot everywhere from a winery in the South of France to vineyards in the central coast of

California and photo studios in New York City. Our photographer, Sara Kerens, has been our go-to since the beginning of Yes Way Rosé. The first time we worked together was in a makeshift "studio" that we fashioned in a well-lit stairwell in Brooklyn. We've all come a long way since then. Sara totally gets us, which is important on set and when traveling together. She makes us feel at ease when we are in front of the camera (not our comfort zone) and has an impeccable eye for detail.

Our planning—and enjoyment—of the process extended beyond assembling our dream team of collaborators. The shot list for the yummy recipe-filled "Are You Readé to Parté" section (see page 110) was scheduled so we could sample the food and drink afterward. We planned recipe photos in the mornings so that we could actually eat the food together as a team for lunch. Cocktails were slotted for the end of the day so we could partake in a few sips. The greatest day, hands down, was when we shot the Yes Way Cheese Tray (see page 139). It was insanely delicious, we all had cheese to take home, and we also photographed it on the same morning as the cake (see page 163). Holé decadence! Sadly, our intern turned out to be allergic to cheese. This was heartbreaking for us, but she was a good sport about it and got out of clean up duté, too.

It's our sincere wish that you find as much joy in reading this book and trying out the recipes as we did putting all of the pieces together. The frosé section is Erica's favorite and has sparked a newfound love for chocolate bitters. Nikki cannot get enough of the astrologé. Her favorite pastime has become sitting around with friends and family and reading them their signs aloud.

We can't wait to see what your favorites are! Tag us @yeswayrose and share how you are making your day Yes Way.

Gratefullé Yours,
Erica + Nikki
@yeswayrose

YES WAY ROSÉ

A Guide to the Pink Wine State of Mind

ERICA BLUMENTHAL + NIKKI HUGANIR

RUNNING PRESS
PHILADELPHIA

Copyright © 2019 Erica Blumenthal and Nikki Huganir
Photography © 2019 Sara Kerens
Illustrations © 2019 Whitney Pollett

Hachette Book Group supports the right to free expression and the value of copyright. The purpose of copyright is to encourage writers and artists to produce the creative works that enrich our culture.

The scanning, uploading, and distribution of this book without permission is a theft of the authors' intellectual property. If you would like permission to use material from the book (other than for review purposes), please contact permissions@hbgusa.com. Thank you for your support of the authors' rights.

Running Press
Hachette Book Group
1290 Avenue of the Americas, New York, NY 10104
www.runningpress.com
@Running_Press

Printed in China

First Edition: April 2019

Published by Running Press, an imprint of Perseus Books, LLC, a subsidiary of Hachette Book Group, Inc. The Running Press name and logo is a trademark of the Hachette Book Group.

The Hachette Speakers Bureau provides a wide range of authors for speaking events. To find out more, go to www.hachettespeakersbureau.com or call (866) 376-6591.
The publisher is not responsible for websites (or their content) that are not owned by the publisher.

Illustrations and photographs copyright Whitney Pollett and Sara Kerens except those on page 14. The images on page 14 are courtesy of the @YesWayRose Instagram account.

Food styling by Maria del Mar Cuadra and prop styling by Chelsea Maruskin.

Library of Congress Control Number: 2018963582
ISBNs: 978-0-7624-9312-8 (hardcover), 978-0-7624-9311-1 (ebook), 978-0-7624-9604-4 (Target Edition)

RRD-S

10 9 8 7 6 5 4 3 2 1

To Nikki. Love, Erica.

To Erica. Love, Nikki.

CONTENTS

OUR STORÉ

Rosé Literallé Changed Our Lives

If we're having a glass of rosé by eleven a.m., we know we're doing something right. This has never been truer than on one sunny, sixty-five-degree morning in the fall of 2017, when we found ourselves in the South of France tasting ten newly harvested rosé blends. The lineup ranged in color from barely there pink to ruby, and the glasses were tinged with flavor profiles from fruit forward to savory. Our mission was to narrow down these options to just one that would become the official Yes Way Rosé wine. After several rounds of tasting and eliminating, we landed on a beautiful, dry, blush-hued rosé with notes of strawberry, citrus, and white peach. In that moment, elated because we knew we were going to have a French wine we absolutely loved as our signature rosé, we jumped up and down and waved our hands in the air in the middle of the winery, dancing like we were at the club. Our dream of creating a wine of our own was finally becoming a realité.

We've been coming up with funny dances together since we were fourteen years old at the small school we both attended in Baltimore. Good friends throughout our formative high school years, we bonded over many things, including a shared crush on Brian Austin Green of *Beverly Hills, 90210* fame. Back then, we never anticipated that fifteen years later we would run a business together.

After going our separate ways for college, we both found our way to New York City. One summer afternoon we ran into each other on the street in SoHo. At that time, Erica was working as a fashion editor at *Jane* magazine, and she helped Nikki land an internship in the design department. We picked up our friendship right where we'd left off, quickly becoming a dynamic duo—if we do say so ourselves—hanging out after work and on the weekends. We had an easygoing rapport and similar interests in fashion, music, and art.

Weekend life back then went a little something like this: Meet for dinner, usually at Lil' Frankie's in the East Village, order wine that we could pronounce, check out a friend's band, and see where the night would take us. At bars and concerts, we ordered Jack and gingers or vodka sodas. We both worked in publishing and lived in New York, so we drank whatever was cheap or, even better, free. What was actually in our glasses was not a priority. Then, everything changed.

Enter rosé.

We wish we could remember the first glass we had, the first bottle we shared, or the first time we joked about our love for rosé. We had no idea that those moments would change our lives forever. We know it was

Without looking for it, we had found our drink *and* our calling.

sometime in 2011, most likely at a Fashion Week party or a café on the Bowery. Archived Gchat conversations (may they rest in peace) indicate that was the year we developed a passion for rosé and began heading to wine stores specifically to buy it.

By the summer of 2012, we were on the brink of obsession, drinking pink wine—always from Provence—almost exclusively. Erica nicknamed rosé "Summer Water" because it went down almost too easily. From there, the rosé puns flowed. An early example: "I'm right on top of that, Rosé," a riff on the 1991 cinematic masterpiece *Don't Tell Mom the Babysitter's Dead.* Coming up with these jokes was a source of endless laughter for us, and our friends couldn't get enough of them. This was the first sign that we were on to something.

At the same time, we sought out restaurants that had rosé on the menu and lamented the fact that it wasn't available at every single place we went. Why didn't our regular spots have a house rosé, we wondered, like the standard red and white? Rosé became our main topic of conversation with anyone who would listen. We just couldn't get past the fact that a drink could be simultaneously so delicious and so beautiful. Plus, we could afford it. Rosé is accessible, even inexpensive, compared to a lot of wine, but it feels luxurious and chic. Just the thought of rosé made us giddy. Without looking for it, we had found our drink *and* our calling. Completely

YES
WAY
ROSÉ

40UNDER40
40UNDER40

infatuated, by summer 2013 we felt compelled to share our love for rosé with the world at large. We took to Instagram, where we could showcase the beauty of rosé, while using our inside jokes as captions to lend a playful voice. A relatively new social media channel, Instagram was still on the rise at that time and not yet a destination for launching brands; it was cool, like something our moms had never heard of. Instagram was the place to let our love of rosé shine for the world, and it was obvious to us that we should use the handle Yes Way Rosé to spread our message on the platform.

From there, everything fell naturally into place: While talking about rosé at a party, as per usual, one friend offered us a perfect tagline in the clever pun "Everything's coming up Rosé." #Summerwater was a shoo-in to be our official hashtag, and for each caption we had a simple test: It had to be breezy and make both of us laugh, just like the wine. This was a creative outlet, an Instagram account—about *rosé* of all things!—and if we were laboring over a caption, it defeated the purpose. Of course, what that purpose was, exactly, was still up in the air.

Soon, though, Yes Way Rosé evolved into something more than witty captions and silly jokes. We began to use our Instagram account to share the names of specific rosés we were drinking, the locations where we were sipping them, and photos of full, pink glasses simply looking gorgeous. Capturing those magic rosé moments became our mission; we brought bottles of wine everywhere so that we never missed a photo opportunité. A shot of the NYC skyline with a glass held up, for example, was the perfect match for the caption "Bright lights, Big rosé." For a bottle on a dusty country trail, we wrote, "Follow the rosé brick road." As pop culture junkies, we worked in references to movies, television, and music whenever possible. For a glass in front of the TV with *The Bachelor* on: "Will you accept this Rosé?"

YES
WAY
ROSÉ
YES
WAY
ROSÉ

That same summer in 2013, Nikki designed our logo, a varsity block letter graphic that boldly stated YES WAY ROSÉ. At the time, a friend of ours had a side hustle printing event totes, and she worked with us to print our new logo on a handful of bags. We thought of it as a way to make what we were doing tangible. The totes, which we of course renamed totés, gave Yes Way Rosé life beyond social media. Instagram was incredibly powerful for our burgeoning brand, but seeing it in real life took it to the next level. Everywhere we went—walking down the street or stepping into elevators—we were stopped by strangers who wanted to know where we bought our bags. There was only one logical next step: to create a website where we could sell the totés to anyone and everyone. Shortly thereafter, we found ourselves meeting early one morning in the county clerk's office at the Manhattan Supreme Court building to obtain a business certificate. Our baby, Yes Way Rosé, was officially born.

Where there's a will, there's a rosé.

In the beginning, mostly people we knew made up our communité of fans, friends, and followers. We grew slowly at first, but we believed in what we were doing and knew that if we built it, the followers would come. We also felt confident that rosé would continue to gain in popularity in the United States, where it could still be hard to come by, especially outside of big cities. It became our mission to spread the rosé word, both for the benefit of others and because we wanted it to be available everywhere you could order a drink. We envisioned going to concerts and ordering rosé instead of beer. We imagined attending summer weddings and being greeted with a cold glass of rosé at the reception. It was a big dream, and reaching that point would require dedication, but we knew we were up to the task—one glass and Instagram post at a time.

It all clicked in May 2014, after Vogue.com interviewed us as rosé

experts for a story called "Why Rosé Is Summer's Most Popular (and Soon-to-Be Most Instagrammed) Drink." This first piece of press gave us credibilité and caught the eye of a special new follower: none other than Drew Barrymore. We had joked about how we thought Drew was the celebrity who best exemplified YWR, with her positive energy and free spirit, and then there she was—our first famous fan. She gave us a shout-out on her Instagram and even posted a photo of herself wearing our sweatshirt while holding a bottle of her Barrymore rosé. Her early support meant the world to us and will never cease to blow our minds.

Clearly, there was a growing interest in what we were doing, and we could sense that the world was finally ready for rosé domination. In the summer of 2014, a wine company approached us about collaborating on a rosé. That conversation led to the first vintage of Summer Water, a delightfully pink wine named in honor of our first joke, which launched in 2015 with a modern label we designed to reflect our strong yet feminine brand. Made in California, that wine became the sip of summer. We were featured on the cover of *Wine Enthusiast Magazine* as influential tastemakers, came out with a nail polish color, expanded our online store, and eventually left our day jobs to pursue Yes Way Rosé full time.

As our empire grew, a big piece of the puzzle was still missing: an official Yes Way Rosé wine, designed by us from start to finish. We explored all of the components needed to create a wine that fully embodied what we love about rosé, from the color and taste down to its affordability. With persistence and luck on our side, we assembled a dream team, made an epic trip to France, and in 2018 released the first vintage of Yes Way Rosé. Dubbed "The French Rosé You Can Actually Say," the classic Provençal-style rosé is super fresh on the inside, stylish and empowered on the outside.

As we've grown Yes Way Rosé, become businesswomen, and followed this surprising path, the one constant amid the craziness has been our commitment to each other as friends. A creative partnership can spark unexpectedly, and we were lucky to find ours one tipsy night together. We can't express after so much hard work, through both growing pains and incredible triumphs, how amazing it felt to dance around in the South of France together.

This book is intended to reflect the sense of love and possibility that is the essence of rosé. We wrote it to shed light on why, like us, you are probably obsessed with rosé. And we wrote it to capture the magic of friendship and support among women, which is so often enjoyed over a glass of the pink stuff. Ultimately, we want to celebrate the moments when, surrounded by besties, you can stop to sip the rosé.

ROSÉ 101

COMPOSITION
BOOK
YES WAY ROSÉ
40 Sheets • 80 Pages
wide ruled with margin
8½ x 7 in/21.5x17.7 cm

YES

Straight É Students

We could talk about wine for hours now, but back when we started Yes Way Rosé, we had close to zero wine knowledge. In the years before embarking on this rosé adventure, we ordered wine in a fairly arbitrary way, with a standard glass of pinot grigio for Nikki and a cabernet for Erica. We didn't have a "signature drink" and became flustered when handed a wine list. Discovering rosé changed all of that. We felt compelled to understand why it was so delicious and what the lingo was so we could feel more confident when it came to ordering. We were able to identify a few commonalities in the wines that captivated us: They were all French rosés from Provence that had a dry taste, had a light pink color, and were served chilled. These characteristics were a good start, but they offered only a hint of what was yet to come.

When we first launched our Instagram in 2013, rosé was booming. Exports from Provence to the United States were growing exponentially, and that same year Angelina Jolie and Brad Pitt released the first vintage of their soon-to-be-everywhere rosé, Miraval. Rosé was becoming ubiquitous, popping up wherever we turned, and we were eager to know more, especially because our friends and followers had begun asking for recommendations. Suffice it to say, we were terrified. We may have come across as authorités on the topic, but we were still only in the early stages of learning.

Our Instagram was based on a connection we had to the wine, a feeling we couldn't articulate at the time. We had no other choice but to educate ourselves. We befriended a sommelier, Meg McNeill, who took us under her wing and graciously let us tag along to tastings with importers. (We became aware of the value of spitting at tastings, but that's a storé for another time. *Pro tip:* Spit.) We immersed ourselves in the culture of rosé, hanging out in wine stores, reading whatever we could on the subject, and traveling to vineyards in Long Island and California. Not a bad way to learn on the job!

Wine is an intimidating subject in general. It's vast and constantly evolving; nature is at play and each year is different. You don't need to become a sommelier to figure out what you like. We are not sommeliers. Our interest is propelled by the incredible places where rosé is made and a desire to know the story behind each bottle. The best advice we can offer is to start with the most beautiful wine out there. Inherently more easygoing than other wines, rosé is the perfect gateway to the wine world. The greatest part? You can sip and learn at the same time.

Fill up a glass and let's get down to the nitté gritté.

A Year in Provence (Rosé)

The circle of life for rosé, from grape to glass, is an annual journé tied to the seasons. The process kicks off in the summer, when Mediterranean heat brings a bounty of grapes to life. The fruit becomes ripe for the picking in fall, when grapes are harvested and then made into wine. During the quiet winter months, the wines are blended and bottled while the vines sleep. Those same vines pick up again in spring, while a fresh crop of grapes bud and the new batches of rosés are happily enjoyed. April showers bring May rosé, and the cycle begins again.

The Éssentials

Rosé:

French (rose-AY), meaning "pink." A centuries-old dry wine that originated in the South of France. Rosé is defined by a distinctive freshness, bright and crisp palate, fruity aromas, and a gorgeous pink color.

Terroir:

French (ter-wahr), translates to "earth." This term encapsulates all of the environmental factors that affect the grapes while they are on the vine, including the climate and the soil in which the grapes are grown. Terroir is the key to everything about wine.

Skin contact:

The sexy part. This is the way both red and rosé wines obtain their color. Grape skins contain almost all of the fruit's pigment, so the pink color of rosé comes from the amount of time the clear juice—made from the colorless pulp of a red grape—spends mingling with the skins. Whereas red wine is made by letting the juice and skins hang out together for a few weeks, or even months, which stains the juice a deep red shade, rosé is usually made with fewer than twenty-four hours of skin contact—a one-night stand, if you will—hence the gorgeous blushing hue that results.

Dry:

As in, not sweet. The relative level of dryness is determined by the amount of residual sugar (RS) in a wine after fermentation. With dry rosés, almost all of the natural grape sugar is converted to alcohol during the fermentation process. This is a quality shared by most of the rosés we personally love. The sensation of "dry" can also come from acidity because acid can counteract sweetness in the proper balance, tricking our senses into reading a wine as dry even if it contains a good amount of RS. Balance is key! When in doubt, demand "dry."

Vintage:

No, we're not talking about a Guns N' Roses tee. In wine terms, *vintage* refers to the year in which the grapes were harvested. The vintage of nearly all still (as opposed to sparkling) rosés is listed on the label and is most likely the year prior to the one in which you're buying it. For example, in 2020 the year on the label of a fresh release will be 2019.

Cuvée:

French (coo-vay), from *cuve*, meaning "tank." This is a tricky one because cuvée has multiple meanings. When it comes to rosé, the most common usage refers to the individual winery's special blend, which might change from year to year, or to a wine made of grapes from one particular plot. A winery may very well release more than one cuvée, and each will go by a different name. For Champagne, the term refers to the high-quality bubbly that comes from the first two thousand liters or so of juice produced when the grapes are first pressed.

Rosétopia

Also known as Provence. It's only fitting that rosé was born in such an idyllic place.

To understand how rosé comes to life, we need to understand its motherland: Provence. The sun-soaked region in southeastern France, commonly referred to as the South of France, is located along the coast of the Mediterranean Sea, bordering the Rhone River and the Languedoc to the west and the Côte d'Azur (French Riviera) and Italy to the east. Provence is a place that conjures all sorts of fantasies and daydreams: Think of it as the place where Beyoncé—all hail the Queen—jumps off the back of a mega yacht while on vacation with Jay-Z and where Leo—no last name needed—parties it up with models and expensive bottles during the Cannes Film Festival. Provence is a picturesque destination known for its wildly fragrant lavender fields, olive groves, and curvy mountain roads. It's the place where Julia Child retreated to the bucolic countryside with her husband, and it was in the Provençal resort town of Antibes that F. Scott Fitzgerald finished *The Great Gatsby.* The perpetual blue sky and breathtaking landscapes have understandably inspired great creativity . . . and rosé masterpieces.

Several of the world's most famous works of modern art were painted in the Provence area. Paul Cézanne, often called "the father of modern art," spent most of his life in his Aix-en-Provence hometown, where he painted a series depicting his favorite landscape, Montagne Sainte-Victoire. A troubled but productive Vincent van Gogh completed *The Starry Night* and *Irises,* among other works, in an asylum in the medieval village of Saint-Rémy-de-Provence. Henri Matisse, who lived most of the time in Nice, conceived and decorated his self-proclaimed masterpiece, *The Rosary Chapel* (also known as "Chapel Matisse"), in the town of Vence, which is

BAR DE LA MARINE
MOBY DICK III

Ancient Historé

Rosé in Provence dates back to around 600 BC, when ancient Greeks founded Massalia (present-day Marseille) in southern France. The Greek settlers brought with them their vines and wines, which were pale in color. The earliest wines were actually closer to pink than to red because the grape skins and juice macerated for only a brief period. (We once heard an unconfirmed rumor that Jesus likely drank rosé. No big deal.)

The Romans, coming through in 125 BC, named the area *Provincia Romana*, now Provence, spread their winemaking techniques, and introduced red wine to the region. Rosé remained popular, though, and during the Middle Ages production increased, encouraged by local winemaking monks, as a revenue stream.

By the fourteenth century, rosé prevailed in Provence and became the wine of choice for the rich and famous, the juice of kings and the aristocracé. Then in the nineteenth century a vicious pest called phylloxera invaded grape vines across Europe, causing incredible devastation; nearly all the vines on the continent had to be grafted onto more resistant roots imported from America before replanting.

Thanks to the railroad and increased tourism in Provence in the twentieth century, rosé had its renaissance. Rosé is now more popular than ever, a popularity that shows no signs of fading. When people call drinking pink a fad, we feel obligated to tell them it's more OG than Ice-T.

filled with his art and magnificent stained-glass windows. And the Spanish pioneer of Cubism and striped shirt enthusiast Pablo Picasso spent the later years of his life working throughout Provence.

Grapevines thrive in the sun, and Provence is blessed with an abundance of vitamin D. With an average of three thousand hours of sunshine per year, the area has weather patterns that rival those of Los Angeles. The winters in Provence are mild, it rarely snows, and the summers are hot and dry. The climate is affected by the mistral winds, a strong, high-pressure force that blows from the northern Alps through the Rhone Valley to the Mediterranean Sea. The powerful winds clear the clouds and dry the air after it rains, helping the vines to stay healthy and averting the mold and rot that can result from excessive moisture.

The soil and geological landscape vary throughout Provence. Rosés growing in the limestone-rich hills of the north and west are influenced by aromatic wild rosemary, juniper, thyme, and lavender plants, collectively termed "garrigue." In the coastal southeast, the soil consists of crystalline rock, and the wines tend to be saltier, thanks to the sea air that breezes through the vineyards.

Grape Expectations

Rosé is made from red wine grape varieties. Let this crucial piece of information sink in for a moment: Rosé is not a mix of red and white wines. Sure, red plus white equals pink, and there are exceptions to the rule, but the method of mixing is really only employed in two instances: (1) Champagne, but we'll get to that; (2) Instagram emergencies.

Whereas any red grape can be used to make rosé, most Provençal rosés are blends of several specific Mediterranean varietals. Rosés from other

regions around the world might also utilize these grapes, or similar ones native to the area, for production:

CABERNET SAUVIGNON: Rich with dark fruit flavors like black cherry and green peppers.

CARIGNAN: A fruit-forward grape with umami notes.

CINSAULT: Refreshing and bright with fresh strawberry notes; primarily used in blends in Provence but stands on its own in some other parts of France.

GRENACHE: Known for its ripe berry fruit flavors, peppery spice, and beautiful light-red color.

MOURVÈDRE: A tannic, muscular varietal with violet floral aromas. This grape is native to Bandol, one of Provence's most prized wine appellations.

SYRAH: Naturally acidic with flavors of blackberry and spice.

TIBOUREN: An earthy and elegantly floral grape found mostly in Provence.

Farm to Glass

These days fresh produce is subject to a lot of different labels. Because wine is an agricultural product, it, too, is frequently described with some confusing language surrounding its origin in the ground. A few different types of special farming certifications are associated with wine production, and different rules and governing bodies exist to administer these certifications in every country.

Of note, however, is that many farmers around the globe have been farming sustainably and organically for centuries, and these days many choose to opt out of the expensive, lengthy, paperwork-heavy process of modern certification; therefore, wines aren't always labeled accordingly. Ask your friendly wine professional for clarification on a bottle if you're curious.

BIODYNAMIC: This method takes into account how the farming affects the Earth and vice versa as well as considers the lunar cycle. It employs some mystical soil treatments and encourages biodiversity in the vineyards, such as planting complementary crops and allowing farm animals to roam among the vines to enhance the health of the soil and of the ecosystem in general.

ORGANIC: The criteria to officially label products as "organic" differs among countries, and even among certifiers, but assume that organic wines have been produced with only naturally occurring, non-genetically modified ingredients in the fields and in the bottle. Any treatments for pests or mold on the vines as well as yeast and preservatives added during winemaking must meet organic standards.

SUSTAINABLE: Farming in a way that benefits not only the current crops but also future crops. Sustainably farmed wine is grown and harvested using minimal chemicals. The methods employed reduce waste and damage to the environment.

Rosé Production

After spending the summer ripening in the hot sun, grapes are ready to be harvested in the autumn. Farmers monitor the vines closely to determine when the grapes have reached peak maturity. The winemaker determines exactly when to pick the fruit on the basis of everything from a scientific measurement of the sugar level in the grapes to a gut feeling had in the middle of the night to the phase of the moon. Harvest in the Northern Hemisphere happens sometime in late August or early September, making the grapes Virgos (just like both of us!). The grapes are picked either by hand or by machine early in the morning while it's still cool, before the hot sun rises and warms them, allowing winemakers to avoid using refrigeration. Keeping the fruit cool is an important part of the winemaking process that stabilizes the sugar and acid levels in the

C34-302HL

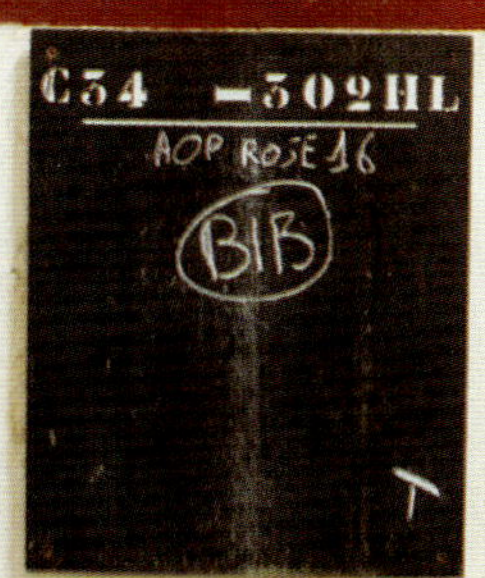
C34 -302HL
AOP ROSE 16
BIB

grapes before pressing. The timing of this picking process is more efficient and less shocking to the delicate grapes, which are then sorted, cleaned, destemmed, and, at this point, several steps closer to finally becoming rosé.

After the grapes are harvested, a few different methods can be employed to produce dry rosés. The first two create what are known as "true rosés" because the grapes have been harvested specifically to make rosé, not red or white wines. The third option is a little more controversial.

Direct Press

In this popular approach, freshly harvested red wine grapes are put into a press and squeezed gently to release a light pink juice. The only exposure the juice has to the skins is during this press, which is why the resulting wine is such a pale color. The juice then flows directly into stainless steel tanks to ferment. Direct pressing uses white-winemaking techniques on red wine grapes to create rosé. Really, it's the best of both worlds. Visualize the process by thinking about how the inside of a grape is clear and the skin is a deep purplish-red. Lightly press together and, voilà, pink!

Limited Skin Maceration

With this method, red wine grapes are crushed with their skins on. The resulting must, which includes the skins, seeds, and stems of the fruit, is then left in a tank to mingle with the clear fruit juices. During this time, the mixture macerates. *To macerate* means to soften by soaking, and for rosé this takes place for a short period of time, generally between two and twenty hours, at a controlled cool temperature. This is when the color, flavor, and tannins of the pigmented skin seep into the juice. Once the liquid is deemed perfectly pink, it is then transferred without the skins into stainless steel tanks to ferment. Red wines are made this way as well, but with a much longer maceration time that leads to a rich berry color, higher alcohol level, and fuller body.

Saignée

A less common method for producing rosé is saignée (pronounced sen-yay), meaning "to bleed" in French, which often results in bolder and darker-hued rosés. This process is used to concentrate red wine, and rosé is essentially created as a by-product. During red wine production, after limited contact with the skins during maceration some of the juice is bled off to ferment separately as rosé. The main batch of juice continues to macerate with the grape must to make red wine. Because the rosé is not intentionally made, but simply a secondary product, it is not considered "true," and the practice of saignée is forbidden in Provence. However,

Tank Girls

Which type of container to use when making and aging a wine is an important decision for a winemaker. Ultimately, the choice depends on the type of wine the producer hopes to create. A wine made in a stainless steel tank will be truer to the flavor of the grapes from which it is made, expressing purer varietal aromas and flavors in its finished form. Because of this clarity of flavor, most rosés are made in stainless steel tanks. Oak barrels, which allow the wine to breathe a bit while it ages, leave a mark on wine, impacting everything from the scent to the flavor. Because rosés, for the most part, don't age in oak, we consider ourselves tank girls for life (and are trying to make #tanklife happen).

C83
100
VT/VP
S:1,8
d=13,36
AT:3,5
C26
VP
08
S 2,1
d 12
C21
AOP
06
S 3,6
d 12,59
At. 3,78

C G
AOP
85
S: 1,3
d: 13,07
At: 3,82
C230
AOP
77
S: 1,9
d: 13,66
At: 3,72
505 Hl
C216
AOP
19
S: 3,1
d: 12,25

it can lead to a delightful rosé completely acceptable in other parts of France and throughout the world.

Whichever way pink is achieved, the resulting juice ferments. Fermentation is the magical process of microorganisms converting sugar to alcohol. It takes place when live yeasts eat the sweet fruit sugar and turn it into alcohol. The yeasts used in this process are often found living and growing naturally on the skins of grapes, but "designer" or specialty yeasts can also be selected to jumpstart the process and add particular flavor components to wines.

Fermentation stops naturally when all of the available sugar has been devoured and the yeast cells starve and die. Any remaining sugar is called residual sugar, or RS, and because not all the sugar can be converted into alcohol, there is always some RS in a wine. Most rosés contain very little RS after fermentation, which is why they tend to be dry rather than sweet. Some winemakers, however, intentionally choose to stop fermentation early to make a sweeter wine, a technique called arrested fermentation. Fermentation can also stop unexpectedly (known as a stuck fermentation)if the yeast dies prematurely, which is usually a highly undesirable outcome.

This accidental event is actually the culprit behind the misconception in America that all rosé is sweet. As the story goes, in 1975 the winemaker at Sutter Home experienced a stuck fermentation during a routine red zinfandel production and decided to release the result anyway: a sweet pink wine they called white zinfandel. Thankfully, America is jumping back on the dry rosé train with the recent rise in the wine's popularity.

The next step on the road to a finished wine, blending, is when things get really fun, because it's when the drinking begins. We've seen winemakers working on a blend look like mad scientists, immersed in the careful process of mixing the different fermented varieties together. The goal of blending is to create a cuvée that is balanced and delicious and that expresses the grapes' terroir. A specific shade of pink can also be obtained through blending, but the intention is generally to capture taste first.

Jean Francois Ott, the fourth-generation winemaker for the legendary French label Domaine Ott, is not fixated on a particular hue, although his wine always seems to turn out an ideal nude-pink shade. "To tell you the truth, I don't really care about the color," he says. "We press a lot of grenache that we cool before and press very gently, so we don't get a lot of color anyway." Blending is why rosés, even those made with the same varieties of grapes from the same regions, result in an array of pink shades and boast a wide assortment of flavors.

Once the wine is bottled, labeled, boxed, and ready to be set free, it is shipped around the world. Bottling is one of our favorite things to watch, and we could enjoy the show for hours. The process involves highly specialized machinery that spins, fills, corks, and labels each bottle as if it were a choreographed dance. Imagine a team of pink Oompa Loompas manning the line and you've got Willé Wonka's Rosé Factory.

Fifty Shades of Rosé

As if we need another reason to be Provence-obsessed, the region is currently home to the world's only research institute dedicated to rosé wine. The Centre de Recherche et d'Expérimentation sur le Vin Rosé, or the Center for Rosé Research, has developed an official color scale for the pink wines of the Provence region. The shades Red Currant, Pink Grapefruit, Peach, Melon, Mango, and Mandarin are meant to serve as a standard point of reference for wine professionals and consumers

alike. We've found the Peach color really speaks to us, and it just so happens to be an almost exact match for our namesake nail polish.

This specific color spectrum refers only to wines from the Provence region; there are plenty of other rosé colors around the world. Because the final shade of a wine depends on so many variables, such as the length of skin contact during pressing and the grape varietals used, the possibilities in the rosé rainbow are infinite. Popular descriptors include a wide range of references, such as onion skin, pink marble, salmon, ruby, and red brick, which are then subject to further clarification depending on their intensité. So, a rosé might appear as a pale coral with flecks of copper, or cotton candy dipped in a pot of rose gold, or even the love child of a flamingo and the *Financial Times* wearing Gwyneth Paltrow's Oscar dress circa *Shakespeare in Love.* It's all subjective.

Don't Judge a Rosé by Its Color

"People shop with their eyes," said Christine Wright, the wine director at New York City's Hearth. "Darker rosés are associated with sweetness, or wines that don't have enough acidity, but that is not always the case." To educate her guests she likes to pour a lighter and deeper rosé side by side, with both options characterized by a bright acidity. "They are often surprised at how much they like the more colorful version." We, too, used to be judgy, specifically when it came to Greek rosés, because they tend to be darker. Now that we know that many of those rosés are dry and elegant—just a little different looking—we feel like we owe them an apologé. (Is it too late now to say sorré?)

Taste the Rainbow with Meg McNeill

Authors' note: We were set up on a friend date with our now rosé BFF Meg McNeill when we were just getting Yes Way Rosé under way, and she's since become our resident expert and pretty much favorite person. She is a sommelier and the owner of Upstream Wines in upstate New York's Livingston Manor, where the rosé selection is plentiful. We asked her to help break down one of the most confusing parts about wine: how to taste it.

There are no wrong answers when it comes to describing what you taste in a glass. All of our taste buds are different and draw from different sensory experiences and memories. That being said, talking about wine can be daunting, and sometimes it helps to have a little vocabulary to draw from when describing the myriad flavors in every bottle of rosé.

A good place to start when tasting a wine is by swirling the liquid a bit in the glass, which releases some of the fragrance. Then take a sniff, keeping your mouth slightly open. What do you smell? Are there floral notes? If so, are they white flowers like lilies, purple flowers like lilac or violet, or are they more pink and rosy? Or perhaps you notice fruit right off the bat. Is that fruit aroma reminiscent of berries, tropical notes, orchard trees, citrus, or stone fruits? Or maybe the smell is something more vegetable, like tomato leaf or bell pepper? Is there anything else? You don't have to mull over this too long; it's not a test. So, let's move on to tasting itself.

Have another sniff of the wine, then take a good sip and hold it in your mouth for a moment before swallowing. If anything stands out right away it's worth noting, but fruit notes are often a good place to start. Is the wine fruity? Is it tart? Hopefully, it's a little of both. Naturally occurring acidity balances out any residual sugar and any strong fruity flavors present in the wine, and it gives rosé that lift at the end that whets your palate and keeps you coming back for more. If you taste berries, think about whether they are ripe or unripe, or more like jam or a pastry. If you are left with more stone fruit tastes, like peaches or apricots, consider whether the taste is fresh-picked, stewed, or even candied. Should you detect strawberries, are they wild or preserved? How about citrus? Is it more like grapefruit or lemons, and is it more like the fruit or maybe the peel? Friendlé reminder: There is no wrong answer.

You can think about flower and plant notes if you find them, or perhaps minerals like sea salt, or the impression of cool river rocks. You

Friendlé reminder: There is no wrong answer.

could detect chemical notes; perhaps the alcohol is a little high or there's the faint taste of sunscreen. (FYI, if you're sipping on the beach, it might just be you.) Diving into the different flavors that make each rosé unique can be enlightening and help in pairing a particular wine with certain foods. But, real talk: This is all optional. You can always skip ahead straight to the drinking part.

Rosé After Labor Day

We are always asked if rosé is a year-round drink. Our official position is that summer may come and go, but rosé is forever! We strongly advocate drinking it throughout the Earth's entire trip around the sun. One of the many remarkable qualities of dry rosé is its versatility when paired with food because it hits the sweet spot between red and white wines with its well-balanced tasting notes. For example, it's the perfect crisp and light choice to sip with heartier meals in the fall, such as Thanksgiving dinner, when flavors are varied. There's also the sheer variety of different blends and styles in the market to give a whirl. Fuller-bodied, richer, more structured rosés in darker hues match well with red meat and winter root vegetables. With many more choices of rosé available now than there are days in the year, one season is simply not long enough to experience them all.

That said, with its undeniable summer appeal, rosé flies off the shelves

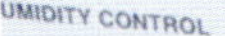

UMIDITY CONTROL

MOËT
CHAMPAGNE
MOËT & CHANDON
ROSÉ IMPÉRIAL

during peak season and some popular cuvées sell out before Labor Day. This is a real tragedé. Thankfully, production of rosé has grown to keep pace with the wine's popularity, and both stores and restaurants now stock and sell rosé throughout the year. Though the options might be more limited during the colder months, industry professionals are increasingly inclined to keep the rosé flowing year-round. Wine pros are eager to show customers more than one style of pink to drink and work to keep devotees happy and hydrated, no matter the weather.

Rosé Within Reach

A most appealing feature of rosé is its wallet-friendly price range. The affordability of this delicious wine initially helped us truly embrace our passion. Wine stores carry classic Provençal rosés for under $15 and more prestigious wines from high-end wineries in the $20 to $25 range. This accessible price point makes the wine more approachable and less precious than fancy reds or whites. If a drop misses the glass or is spilled on the deck of a boat or a dance floor, it is not cause for despair. From the first glass, we connected to the unpretentious nature of rosé. Even on a budget, one can drink it in abundance and sample multiple labels. Of course, splurge-worthy rosés are available, as are $20 glasses on restaurant wine lists. Yes Way Pay Day! Mostly, though, trying new rosés can be delicious and elevated while remaining cost-effective.

Pop Till You Drop

Our hearts burst with love when it comes to rosé bubbles. Sparkling wine has a special way of making any moment feel glamorous, and when it's pink—forget about it. Although it has a reputation as the go-to for New Year's Eve and wedding toasts, bubblé need not be reserved for special occasions. Nor does it need to be served strictly in a fancy flute or coupe. We often take ours casually in a stemless wine glass, out of a can, or even in a Solo cup. Popping a bottle of sparkling rosé is like putting on the most fabulous accessory, or bright-red lipstick, that instantly turns a T-shirt and jeans into a dashing parté-readé look. Yes Way Bubblé!

Bubblé 101

There are a few ways to put the bubbles in a bottle of bubblé. The traditional method, also known as *méthode champenoise,* dates back to the 1690s. The story goes something like this: A Benedictine monk by the name of Dom Perignon invented Champagne in the French region of the same name, which remains the only place in the world legally allowed to call its sparkling wine "Champagne." In the traditional method of vinification, another word for winemaking, bubbles are created through a secondary fermentation in the bottle. This exact process is utilized by sparkling winemakers in other regions around the world, though the wine, and even the method, goes by different names. It can get a little confusing, but as Ariel Arce, the owner of Air's Champagne Parlor in New York, clarifies succinctly: "Any [bubbly] wine made from any place outside of Champagne is considered sparkling wine." In other parts of France, for example, the *méthode champenoise* is referred to as the Crémant method and the bottles produced are labeled "Crémant." In Penedès, Spain, an identical technique is used to make Cava. Certain bottles of bubbly in Italy go by *Franciacorta,* which, similar to Champagne, is the name given to both the wine and the region that produces it. And, from California to the Hamptons, great American wineries are producing high-quality sparkling using the traditional method, often for a fraction of the price of Champagne—with results that are arguably just as festive.

The fastest-selling everyday bubbles come in the form of Prosecco —an affordable Italian-style sparkling wine. Despite this popularity, it is important to know that the powers that be in that wine's particular region have wine laws that prohibit the making of Prosecco in rosé form; therefore, nothing pink is actually labeled "Prosecco." (Authors' note: At the

YES

time of publication it was reported this law may be changing, so this may no longer be true! Please don't sue us if so.)

You will, however, find sparkling rosés from the same Italian region, and even from the same producers, as your favorite Prosecco. In this case, rosé bubbles by any other name are just as sweet (er, dry). These sparklers are made in the Charmat method or tank method, in which the bubble-producing secondary fermentation occurs in large stainless steel tanks. The bubbles produced here are small and delicate, and when bottled, the pressure is about half that found in a bottle of bubbles made in the traditional method.

Champagne

The exception to the rule of not mixing red and white wines to make pink occurs with Champagne, where mixing is the most widely used technique to make sparkling rosé. First things first, though—there are three grapes primarily used for Champagne: Pinot Noir (red), Chardonnay (white), and, less commonly, Pinot Meunier (red). After the red and white grapes go through their first fermentation, the resulting still wines are combined in a process known as *Rosé d'assemblage,* in which a small percentage of pinot noir is blended into a chardonnay base. Rosé Champagne can also be made with red grapes alone via the saignée method (described on page 40), in which some of the juice is bled off after a short maceration and fermented separately to become rosé wine. Regardless of method, the resulting pink juice is then made effervescent during a second fermentation inside the bottle, which is tipped off by added yeast and sugar. When the yeast consumes the sugar contained in the bottle, it releases carbon dioxide, blessing the liquid with bubbles. From there, a few key

Absolutelé Fabulous

Champagne is dominated by big, high-fashion producers, and luxury brands with luxury price tags. These beloved and decadent sparklers are made from fruit grown in several vineyards, often purchased from different farmers who specialize in growing grapes, not making wine, throughout the approved Champagne region. The selected grapes are then blended to maintain consistency and high quality across the brand's offerings. "Grower" Champagne refers to a farm-to-table style in which the winery that grows the grapes makes the wine, too. Many of these one-stop-shop Champagne houses have been operated by the same families for generations. With grower Champagne, you are likely to sense the terroir of a specific, smaller subregion as well as a particular style that is unique to that place and label. The choice between a fancy name brand and a lesser-known boutique bottle is a win-win because in all likelihood the bubbles will be exceptional in both cases.

steps are strictly followed to make the bubbly pink stuff into Champagne:

AGING ON LEES: "Lees" is code for dead yeast cells, a by-product of the second fermentation. The wine ages on the lees (meaning, with those dead cells) for fifteen months for nonvintage wines and three years for vintage.

To note: Champagnes are either nonvintage, made of grapes harvested in different years, or vintage, made with grapes harvested all in the same year.

RIDDLING: A process in which the bottles, stored at an angle, are turned regularly, which moves the dead yeast cells to the neck of the bottle.

CHAMPAGNE
Paul Laurent
CHAMPAGNE
Paul Laurent
Cuvée du Fondateur
BRUT ROSÉ
UNDERWOOD
11% ALC./VOL.
375 ML
2016
eXile
Lise & Bertrand JOUSSET
Rosé pétillant
VIN DE FRANCE
12% vol. - 750ml
Contains sulfites - Product of France

DISGORGEMENT: This procedure involves freezing the neck of the bottle to release the yeast sediment.

DOSAGE: Grape sugar from still wine, which can vary in sweetness, is added to the Champagne. The sugar level in the dosage wine determines the sweetness of the final product.

CORKING: The last step! A mushroom-shaped cork is inserted into the bottle and secured with a wire cage without which the pressure inside the bottle could force the cork out at the slightest provocation. In this instance, it's best to keep things bottled up inside.

Pét-Nat

Pétillant-naturel, a phrase meaning "natural sparkling" and commonly abbreviated to *pét-nat,* used to be the hipster cousin to Champagne. Now going mainstream, think of *pét-nat* as the skinny jeans of bubbles —a former niche item that is soon to be widespread. *Pét-nat* is made using the ancestral method, which generates soft sparkling wine by bottling the juice when it is only partially fermented. The wine is, in effect, still alive. With carbon dioxide trapped in the bottle, bubbles form as fermentation finishes. *Pét-nats* are predominantly unfiltered wines and appear a touch cloudy because the disgorging process is eliminated in this type of winemaking, thus leaving sediment in the bottle. These unique bottles are also topped with a "crown cap," much like the cap you find on a beer bottle, instead of a traditional cork. Whereas Champagne making is precise and controlled, these wines are wild and unpredictable. No yeast or sugar is added to jump-start fermentation, resulting in a real element of surprise in the finished wine. The final product can be funky like hard cider, dry and effervescent, or slightly sweet. Choosing a bottle is sort of like going on a blind date: You hope for the best, and regardless of whether you meet your soul mate or a dud, at least you have a story to tell.

The Must-Have Tool

Of all of the wine gadgets on the market, our favorite is a Champagne stopper. Preserving a bottle of bubbly for another day or two takes the pressure off (pun intended) finishing the contents in one sitting and makes the bottle transportable after opening.

How to Safelé Open Bubblé

Avoid an injuré, to yourself or others, with these quick steps:

1. Unwind the cage with six half-turns. In the formal style of opening a bottle, the cage stays on throughout opening.

2. Hold the bottle at a 45-degree angle and grab the bottom in one hand while applying pressure to the cork and cage with the other. Hold on for dear life.

3. Turn the base of the bottle—not the cork—still at an angle, until it pops into your tightly clenched hand. Pour into a glass or directly into your mouth.

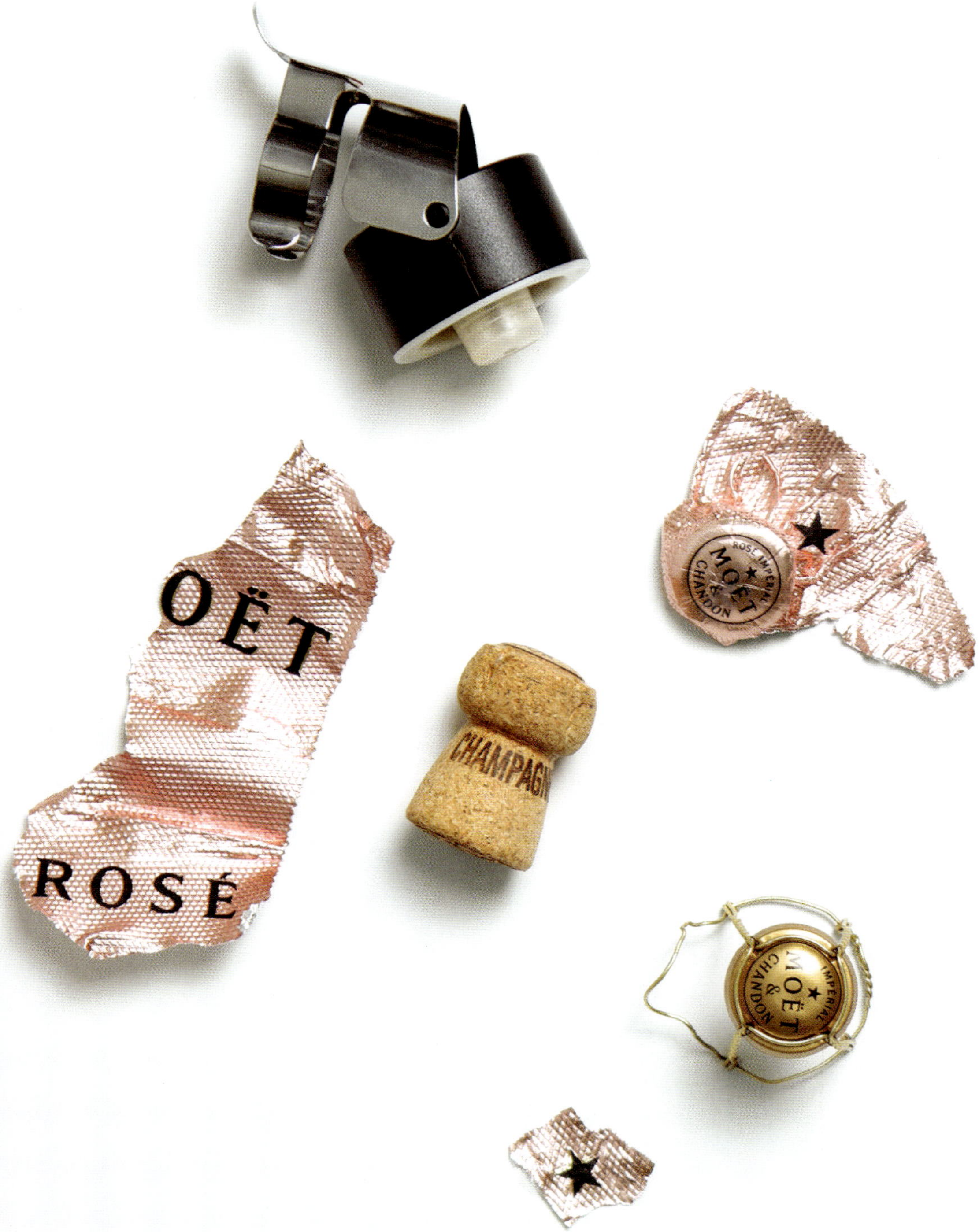
OËT
ROSÉ
CHAMPAGN
ROSE IMPERIAL
MOËT & CHANDON
IMPERIAL
MOËT & CHANDON

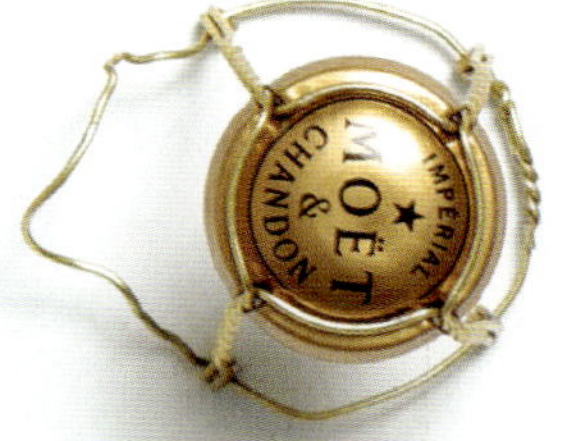

Rosé Geographé

Any red wine–producing region is able to make rosé, too. From New York to New Zealand, different styles are produced using varietals specific to the region's terroir. Every time we open a bottle of rosé, whether it hails from Hungary, Patagonia, or perhaps Slovenia, we feel like we're being transported to that happé place. Join us as we take a trip around the world with rosé.

North Atlantic Ocean
Labrador Sea
Hudson Bay
NUNAVUT
MANITOBA
QUEBEC
LABRADOR
ONTARIO
UNITED STATES
Bermuda Islands
United Kingdom
Lesser Antilles
BAHAMAS
Gulf of Mexico
Straits of Florida
CUBA
Havana
HAITI
JAMAICA
Greater Antilles
Caribbean Sea
MEXICO
Mexico City
Guadalajara
BELIZE
Belmopan
HONDURAS
Tegucigalpa
NICARAGUA
Managua
GUATEMALA
San Salvador
EL SALVADOR
San Jose
COSTA RICA
PANAMA
COLOMBIA
Bogota
VENEZUELA
Caracas
GUYANA
SURINAME
FRENCH GUIANA
ECUADOR
Quito
PERU
Lima
BOLIVIA
La Paz
BRAZIL
Brasília
AMAZON BASIN
Manaus
PARAGUAY
Asuncion
ARGENTINA
CHILE
Galapagos Islands
Revillagigedo Is.
[Mexico]
Clipperton (France)
Los Angeles
San Diego
San Francisco
Las Vegas
Phoenix
Denver
Dallas
Houston
New Orleans
Miami
Orlando
Tampa
Jacksonville
Atlanta
Nashville
Memphis
St. Louis
Chicago
Toronto
Montreal
Ottawa
Boston
New York
Philadelphia
Washington D.C.
Winnipeg
Calgary
Edmonton
Vancouver
Seattle
Salt Lake City
Oklahoma City
Kansas City
Louisville
Cleveland
Detroit
Minneapolis
St. Paul
Milwaukee
Buffalo
Norfolk
Charleston
Savannah
Jacksonville
John F. Kennedy Space Center
Nassau
Santiago de Cuba
Santo Domingo
Port-au-Prince
Kingston
PUERTO RICO
DOMINICAN REP.
Port of Spain
TRINIDAD & TOBAGO
Georgetown
Paramaribo
Cayenne
Barranquilla
Cartagena
Maracaibo
Medellin
Cali
Guayaquil
Cuenca
Iquitos
Trujillo
Chiclayo
Arequipa
Cuzco
Santa Cruz
Porto Velho
Santarém
Belém
Fortaleza
Recife
Salvador
Monterrey
Chihuahua
Hermosillo
Tijuana
Acapulco
Oaxaca
Veracruz
Puebla
León
Tampico
Mérida
Yucatan Pen.
Baja California
Gulf of California

Provence

Viticultural Provence is broken down by appellations, called AOCs (short for *appellations d'origine contrôlée*), a strict French governmental system that identifies where a wine is made geographically and specifies what quantities of which grapes can be used and the allowed alcohol percentage (in the finished wine) by volume. Provence has nine AOCs. The Côtes de Provence, or CDP, to be cute, is the largest, most internationally known of the group. Popular global labels such as Chateau des Esclans Whispering Angel, Chateau Miraval, and Commanderie de Peyrassol are all Côtes de Provence bottlings. Each cuvée is different, but these wines tend to be delicate, bone dry, and delicious, with fresh fruit notes and bright acidity.

Bandol is a seaside town in Provence and an appellation of its own, known for producing the region's most highly regarded red wines and age-worthy rosés using the spicy Mourvèdre grape. Bandols are more robust than classic Provençal rosés, and our choice for winter rosé drinking. Monsieur Ott, the winemaker for the iconic Domaine Ott, says that in the winter he drinks Bandol rosés of vintages dating back as many as three years. This is one rosé that really benefits from a little time lingering in the bottle. The town is also home to the most famous of all the rosés: Domaine Tempier Bandol, a benchmark rosé with a romantic history. Lucie "Lulu" Tempier and her winemaking husband, Lucien Peyraud, were gifted her family's wine estate, Domaine Tempier, for their wedding in 1936. Celebrated by legendary food and wine figures, every vintage of this vibrant, biodynamic rosé is a new chapter in an everlasting love story.

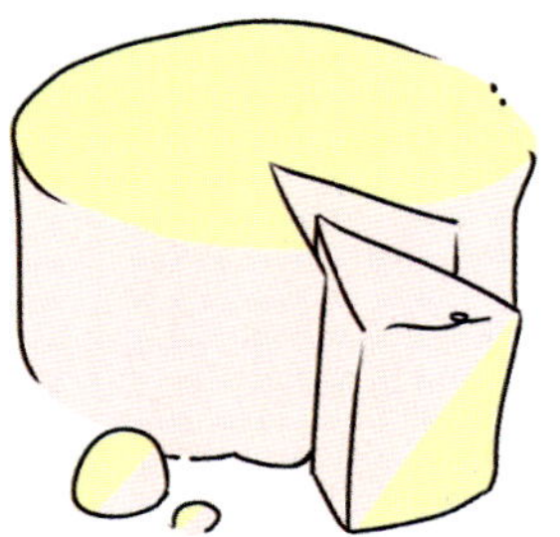

France: Rosé Beyond Provence

In Burgundy, the prestigious homeland of pinot noir and chardonnay, some rosés are produced in the northern village of Marsannay. In addition to enjoying the Pinot Noir–based, red-fruit taste of these wines, we like that it sounds fancy to drink wine from Burgundé. South of Burgundy is Beaujolais, the region famous for its young red wines, where tasty rosés are made with tart and light-bodied Gamay grapes. In the diverse Loire Valley in central France, a variety of refreshing pink styles are produced, including aromatic and minerally Sancerre rosés made with Pinot Noir, and elegant, slightly spicy Chinon rosés made from Cabernet Franc.

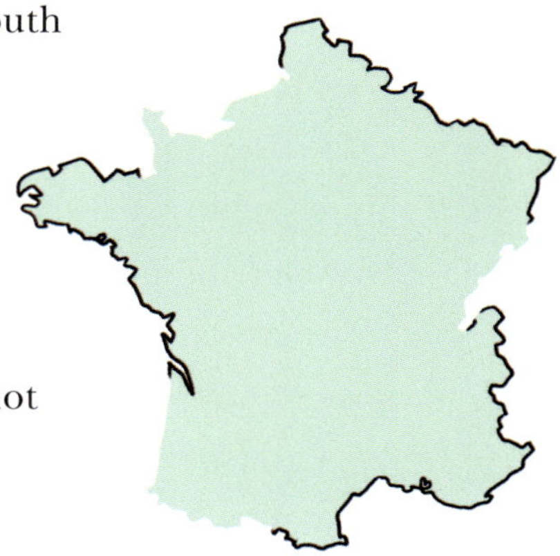

Tavel in the southern Rhone Valley is an appellation dedicated entirely to making seriouslé dry rosé—sort of like us. Tavel rosés are a touch darker than other wines and are believed to improve with age, an opinion that the French novelist Honoré de Balzac allegedly shared. We can certainly relate to aging gracefully. In the Languedoc-Roussillon, Provence's neighbor in southern France, juicy, often affordable rosés that taste of ripe summer fruit are mostly made using the same grapes as classic Provençal blends.

Take a ferry to Corsica from the South of France for standout rosés ideal for an island getaway. Crisp and bone dry, these wines are blended from local red wine grape varietals: Niellucciu, Barbarossa, and Sciacarello. Rosé gold star if you ace those grape name pronunciations after a glass or two!

Spain

Pass the paella and a glass of rosado (with a *D*) in España. Provence may be the motherland of rosé, but the grapes most widely used there originated in Spain. Monastrell is the Spanish name for Mourvèdre, and Garnacha, aka Grenache, actually first came from Spain as well. Navarra, in the north of the country, is known for refreshingly punchy Garnacha-based rosados. In neighboring Rioja, the pink wines are blended with the choice Tempranillo grape as well as a tiny little bit of the white grape Viura from a few super-traditional producers like Muga and Ostatu. We know we said that doesn't happen with dry rosé, but there have to be some rosé rebels, right? Up north in the Basque region, Txakolina (pronounced chak-o-leena) rosé boasts a prickly effervescence and vibrant acidity, the perfect wine to pair with the region's inventive tapas before an afternoon siesta.

Italy

You say *tomato,* I say *rosato* (with a *T*). Distinctive rosés are produced all over Yes Way Italé. In the northern Italian town of Bardolino, they make a pale, dry rosé called chiaretto. Lively and tannic, these wines are primarily a Corvina and Rondinella blend, incorporating the same grapes used to make the region's high-end amarone wine. We visited the area recently and stayed near Lake Garda, a breathtaking place featured in a scene from the film *Call Me by Your Name,* and drank chiaretto with every kind of tortellini and risotto imaginable. Over in Piedmont, Nebbiolo, the same grape that makes bold (and baller) Barolo and Barbaresco makes a sophisticated rosé fit for the famous wild truffles foraged nearby. Under the Tuscan sun, Sangiovese rules supreme and makes an extremely food-friendlé rosato to pair with endless antipasti. In the south, Sicilian Nero D'Avola and Nerello and Pugliese Primitivo are used to create fuller-bodied, dramatic rosato to drink with rich meats and heavy spices. *Mamma mia,* we're hungré just thinking about it.

Hungary, Austria, and Germany

We were surprised to learn that rosé is the most popular style of wine in Hungary, where it receives all the respect we think it rightfully deserves. Wineries there produce a variety of rosés, ranging from the faintly sweet to very, very dry—showcasing the wine's versatility for food-pairing purposes. Winemaker Tamás Dúzsi, known as the "King of Rosé," makes a whole spectrum of different styles of serious pink wine that he exports across the world, to the delight of his many thirsté subjects—us included. Farther up the Danube River, producers in Austria build sturdy, acid-driven rosés from the widely planted Zweigelt grape and fruity, lush numbers from St. Laurent (the grape, not the French fashion house).

After a quick trip on the Eurail to Germany, you might pair your schnitzel with a Spätburgunder rosé. German for Pinot Noir, Spätburgunder is grown across the country's wine regions; in fact, Germany is the third largest producer of pinot in the whole world. Weingut Von Winning's organic rosé, from the Pfalz region, is perfectly balanced and a superior match for sausages and kraut.

Fresh rosé and sunny days are pretty good reasons to cross the equator.

Rosé South of the Equator

Hot tip: When it's winter in the Northern Hemisphere and the vines are sad and bare, play snowbird and head to lands down under where it's full-on summer and the new vintage of rosés is just being released. Fresh rosé and sunny days are pretty good reasons to cross the equator. In the Patagonian mountains of Argentina, intense, fuchsia, slightly tannic rosés made from Malbec rule and easily stand up to the impressive stacks of meat you'll encounter in Mendoza. And in Australia, vibrant Shiraz rosés are the wines to sip while chasing kangaroos, gorging on barbecue, and surfing some of the most beautiful waters in the world.

U.S.É.

Our home turf, the United States, is full of relatively young winemaking regions, mostly pioneered by European immigrants. Unencumbered by centuries of traditions, American winemakers enjoy a freedom to play around and experiment with different grapes and new, invigorating techniques.

A case in point is one of our rosé obsessions, Love Drunk, made by sommelier-winemaker André Houston Mack in Oregon's Willamette Valley.

LORENZA
ROSÉ 2017
CALIFORNIA

WÖLFFER ESTATE
SUMMER IN A BOTTLE

LOVE
DRUNK

We were first drawn to this unexpected Champagne-inspired blend of chardonnay and pinot noir with notes of watermelon and kiwi because of its graphic label. We had the good fortune of discovering this wine around the time Beyoncé's classic "Drunk in Love" was released, and we were never tired (never tired) of sipping it all night. Another standout from the Pacific Northwest is Division, a cool, urban winery owned by a couple of Francophiles in Portland that sources sustainably grown grapes from around the region for their still and sparkling rosés. These winemakers explore unique varietals and progressive techniques, and throw killer parties, Portlandia style, with inventive food and good vibes.

All over sunny California, the rosé is flowing. Napa cabernet sauvignon and Sonoma pinot noir are red wines that have earned worldwide respect and often come with hefty price tags. Luckily, serious red wine grapes also make delicious rosés. Cabernet tends to be a little edgier with a spicy finish, while pinot will generally offer soft fruit and bright acidity. We're California dreamin' for our favorites from Sonoma's Scribe and Red Car wineries. A number of producers in the Napa area, including Wind Gap, Sinskey, and Jolie-Laide, make their rosé from pinkish grapes like Pinot Gris and Trousseau Gris—gray-skin varieties—that, when left in contact with the juice, give the resulting wine the most beautiful rose-quartz hues and a light, delicate palate. Some innovative young producers are embracing this old-world technique, and we can't get enough of it.

We learned about great Provence-inspired Californian rosés in the early stages of Yes Way Rosé when we met Melinda Kearney and Michele Ouellet, a mother-daughter team from St. Helena in Napa who have been using traditional

varietals from old vines to make their always delightful Lorenza rosé since 2008. Farther south, the savory rosés from Santa Barbara and the surrounding Central Coast, which we call the Provence of California, pick up a certain freshness from the Pacific breeze, calling to mind coastal Mediterranean bottles. We take any and all California rosés with a Beach Boys soundtrack, or Tupac, and classic Cali cuisine like avocado toast and In-N-Out burgers.

On the East Coast, New York State winemakers are also thinking pink. Wölffer Estate on Long Island makes a number of quick-to-sell-out rosés in Provençal styles that are dreamy for a Hamptons beach weekend. Upstate in the Finger Lakes region, cool-climate Cabernet Franc and Pinot Noir go into refined bottles best appreciated sitting on the dock of the bay.

We find that American producers excel at not taking wine too seriouslé and remembering that rosé should be fun. The plethora of canned rosés now available is a prime example of this playful attitude. California's Paper Planes, Oregon's Underwood, and Long Island's Bridge Lane have all embraced this grab-and-go format that is ideal for any outdoor activité.

Where in the World Is Jordan Salcito?

A wine authorité with impeccable taste, Jordan Salcito has traveled pretty much everywhere tasting rosé. The director of Special Wine Projects for Momofuku, this busy woman has also managed to create both a modern wine cooler company, Ramona, and the wine brand Bellus. We're honored that she shared with us a few of her favorite rosés from around the world.

SANDHI WINES STA. RITA HILLS BRUT NATURE ROSÉ, SANTA BARBARA, CALIFORNIA

"Winemaker Rajat Parr made this wine in collaboration with Michael Cruse, the man behind nearly every compelling bottle of sparkling wine to come out of California this century. It embodies so many of

the things I love about wine: collaboration, experimentation, a commitment to excellence, and of course sensational taste. This wine, primarily made from Chardonnay with a tiny amount of Pinot Noir blended for color, is produced in the traditional method."

BODEGA CHACRA, MAINQUE ROSÉ, RIO NEGRO, PATAGONIA

"Winemaker Piero Incisa della Rochetta's vision for Chacra, his biodynamic vineyard and farm in Rio Negro, Patagonia, is a wine-related story I adore. The grandson of a world-famous winemaker, Piero was born in Italy but developed a profound affection for Burgundy's wines. After visiting a cousin in Patagonia, Piero discovered some old, extremely rare ungrafted Pinot Noir vines, bought a plot of land, built a winery, and has begun crafting profound Pinot in Argentina. This rosé is compelling and pure, beautifully made, and biodynamically farmed."

CLOS CIBONNE CUVÉE SPÉCIALE DES VIGNETTES, PROVENCE, FRANCE

"This Provençal rosé is hardly what one envisions when considering wines in this category. One of those rare rosés that almost behaves like a red, this wine feels more appropriate in fall or winter, with a roast chicken or black truffles, than in summer, with sunshine and beach hair. Made from Tibouren, an ancient grape of which Julius Caesar was supposedly a fan, this wine is fermented, then aged under a layer of 'fleurette' (a thin veil of yeast) in one-hundred-year-old foudres (large wooden barrels). The result is an earthy, otherworldly expression of rosé that is worth keeping around all year long."

ROSÉ VIBES ONLÉ

Uncovering what makes rosé so extraordinaré became our mission when we realized what a powerful influence it was having on every aspect of our lives. We wondered why rosé made us constantly crack up, especially when we weren't even drinking. Why were we suddenly wearing pink, when we aren't exactly girly girls? We even tried learning French in the service of our love for the pink stuff (mission incomplete). Rosé was consuming most of our thoughts and had turned us into pink people. To be honest, we were both funnier and all-around happier once we embraced this rosé state of mind. At that point we knew that things had gone far beyond an interest in wine.

Our epiphané was the realization that the unique qualities of rosé inspire endless joy. The color and taste, as well as how it's made, served, and sipped, symbolize an ideal pink-tinted dream world, where friendship and humor rule. In this blush universe, it's often the little things that are cause for celebration. There are high fives all around when you find a shady parking spot at the beach, and then again when you easily find your car on the way out. Dance parties break out before you get to the dance party. Fits of laughter are a form of ab work. Friends are empowered to build empires together over a glass of rosé.

The carefree feelings inspired by this pink philosophé are what we call "rosé vibes." They can be found all around you, even sans rosé, and with them by your side, the glass is always more than half full. The cup actually overfloweth.

Tickled Pink

The first thing you notice about rosé is that *pink*. The color is intoxi-catingly beautiful. Classic rosés are a translucent hue, somewhere in between peach and blush. More flesh tone than bubblegum, it's a feminine and cheeky shade, the color your face turns when you bump into your cute neighbor or a crush slides into your DMs. This gorgeous liquid has the ability to, figurativelé, create sunshine on a cloudy day.

Rosé changed our personal styles. We both had absolutely no pink in our closets before Yes Way Rosé. Our New York wardrobes consisted mostly of black, denim, and gray. When this romantic shade appeared in our lives, it became our new neutral. The sophisticated, almost noncolor allowed us to brighten up and match our looks to our new rosier attitudes. For the first rosé event we ever hosted, a tasting at Dandelion Wine in Brooklyn,

we dressed the part. It was our parté and we'd wear rosé if we wanted to! The amount of pink in our present-day lives is almost comical, but we wouldn't have it any other way. Pink has infiltrated our home decor, cookware, and luggage—and if you'd like a pick-me-up in your life, we highly recommend letting it infiltrate yours. We've found the hue provides a subtle way to add more joy to daily routines.

Generation Rosé

When we launched Yes Way Rosé in 2013, pink was on the brink of a color explosion. There was a quick and radical shift toward light pink in fashion and beauty, as new chic labels, such as Glossier and Mansur Gavriel, began using blush tones for their branding. Pink gradually took over Instagram feeds, runways, and even technology, with Apple releasing a rose-gold iPhone in 2015. Pantone named rose quartz the Color of the Year in 2016 and the phenomenon now known as millennial pink became rampant. The ever-influential Rihanna seemed to only wear pink, with each glamorous ensemble more fabulous than the next; everyone was dyeing their hair various shades of pink, including us; and pink became the choice hue for book covers and restaurant interiors. Men wanted in, too, and the *New York Post* ran a cover photo of President Obama holding a blush sweater in the Gap with the headline "I'll take the pink one." Hit maker Drake even used it for his wildly popular and often imitated "Hotline Bling" artwork. So, which came first, the rosé or the trend? We'll always contend that the wine played a big part in the rapid rise of the rosy shade.

Complementaré Color Wheel

In case you missed that day of kindergarten, complementary colors sit across from one another on the color wheel, having opposing qualities on the light spectrum and canceling each other out when mixed together. However, paired with another complementary tone, they create the most aesthetically pleasing duo, with both colors actually appearing brighter. The many tints of rosé varietals are in the red family, making them fittingly complementary to those of nature's numerous shades of green. Next time you pour a glass, use this handé tool to find your rosé's most eligible mate.

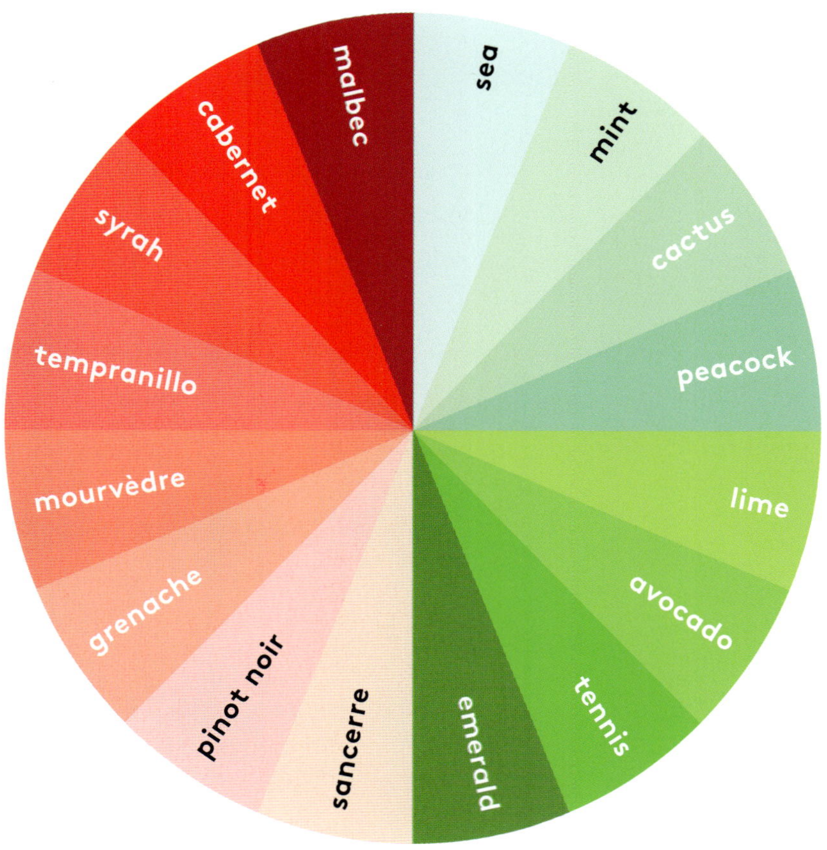

Rosé on the Dailé

Just as a glass of rosé can elicit happiness, so can a healthé dose of pink. Our tips for how to inject a pop into your life follow the mantra that a little goes a long way.

- While drinking at the office is mostly frowned upon, there are plenty of ways to spice up your workday with color. Keep a light pink notebook, pen, or sticky notes on your desk for strong rosé vibes. This may result in a promotion-worthy new idea.
- Drink water out of rosé-colored glasses. If you aren't drinking a glass of rosé, it should at *least* look like one.
- We touch our phones countless times a day, and you are probably touching yours right now, too. Snap on a rosé case and elevate your mood every time you refresh.
- There is nothing better or more essential in the dead of winter than a big, cozy sweater. Oh wait, there is. When the fluffy sweater is a light shade of pink, it can make trudging through the snow feel like floating on a happé cloud.
- Hit the hay in rosé. Go wild with all-pink bedding for blush-tinged dreams. If that's too much, a rosy blanket or accent pillow will also make for a good night's sleep.

PENCIL ERASER
ecoStick
instax

Chill

What's cooler than being cool? Rosé. This is a casual wine, a beverage to sip chilled, literallé, while at your chillest. Most bottles of rosé come with screw caps for this reason, to enhance the breezy attitude. Twisting off the top is like cracking open a cold one, only it's rosé instead of beer and much easier on the eyes. With a twist top, you don't have to worry about any cork breakage or having to fit a misshapen cork back into the bottle. Trust us when we say we've been there. Plus, screw caps keep the wine fresh for longer because less air creeps in. How chill is that?

The ultimate rosé drinking experiences are similarly effortless. There's really nothing quite like sharing a cold bottle, glistening with condensation, on a long sun-kissed beach day with your crew. Or bumping into a friend and having an impromptu glass that leads to a second and makes the world

feel like your oyster. This lightheartedness sets rosé apart. We relish the rosé days of summer when a bottle is always on ice.

Stay Cool

Rosé is served cold to complement the wine's light body and the hot weather that occurs when it is most frequently enjoyed. Serving a rosé too warm, or even too cold (yes, that's a thing), can change the way it tastes and smells. The ideal temperature for serving is between 45 and 55 degrees Fahrenheit, not ice cold but cooled down just enough. The method to get a bottle to this temperature, however, depends on what's available.

REFRIDGERÉTION: A no-brainer. Room temperature bottles need roughly an hour in the fridge to cool down.

FLASH FREEZE: When in a rush, pop a bottle in the freezer, where it takes about thirty minutes to cool down. Do not forget to take your bottle out or you could go from yes way to no rosé because of an explosion.

ROSÉ ON ICE: A single ice cube works wonders to cool down a glass.

OTHER: On a cool night, it's like, whatever, man. Leave it on a windowsill, in the garage, or on the patio. No worries.

The Chill Factor

Because rosé doesn't need to be taken so seriouslé, it should be enjoyed in a variety of formats. Rosé can be found in all shapes and sizes to suit any situation, from a black-tie wedding to a sunset stroll.

YES WE CAN: The easiest way to transport rosé or sneak it into a movie is in a can. Accessorized with kooziés, they are even more lovable.

C'EST CLASSIQUE: The little black dress of wine vessels, a typical 750-milliliter bottle of rosé is classic goodness.

LARGE AND IN CHARGE: Magnums, which contain twice the volume of a regular bottle, come in handé when you're always reaching for the next bottle.

ROSÉ IN A BOX: A 3-liter box holds four bottles' worth of rosé and is ideal for wherever glass is a nonstarter.

BIG DADDÉ: A jeroboam makes an unforgettable entrance. We once showed up to a party with this gigantic bottle, 4.5 liters or equal to six standard bottles, and have never lived it down.

MOTHER OF ALL: The standard wine keg holds twenty-six bottles, so you better have one epic rager planned for this bad boy.

Yes Way Moviés

Watch Netflix and chill with the top pink films ever made. In order chronologicallé:

1. *Funny Face* (1957): Starring Audrey Hepburn, this musical features a fabulous number called "Think Pink" in which Kay Thompson, as the editor in chief of *Quality* magazine, declares pink the new "color of the season." Some things never change.

2. *Grease* (1978): From the Pink Ladies and Frenchie's beauty-school drop-out hair to Danny's *Born to Hand Jive* dance shirt, this summer-lovin' story is full-on rosé vibes.

3. *Pretty in Pink* (1986): The iconic eighties high school flick written by John Hughes stars Molly Ringwald as Andie, a girl from the wrong side of the tracks who wears pink exclusivelé. Our childhood favorite, it gave both the color and DIY prom dresses a cool punk edge.

4. *The House of Yes* (1997): In this dark comedé, Parker Posey plays a Jackie

HOLLYWOOD
PRODUCTION ROSÉ VIBES ONLÉ
DIRECTOR YES WAY ROSÉ
CAMERA MY PHONE
DATE
SCENE
TAKE

Fresh!

O–obsessed young woman recently released from a psychiatric hospital, pink Chanel suit and all.

5. *Legally Blonde* (2001): When people ask us what we think of orange wine, Elle Woods and this legendary zinger come to mind: "Whoever said orange is the new pink is seriously disturbed."

6. *Mean Girls* (2004): This (Yes Way) Tina Fey–scripted masterpiece was clearly about rosé lovers in the making. On Wednesdays, they wear pink.

7. *Marie Antoinette* (2006): As directed by the namesake of Francis Ford Coppola's Sofia Rosé, the indulgent queen's famous quote may as well have been "Let them drink rosé!"

8. *Bridesmaids* (2011): Kristen Wiig and Rosé Byrne are out of control funny as rivals in this movie that will forever be hysterical for an insanelé drunk airplane scene.

9. *The Grand Budapest Hotel* (2014): Pink is frequently used for the whimsical sets of Wes Anderson's movies, but he takes it to another level in this charming film. From the hotel building's exterior to the prop newspapers and pastry boxes, the color is the star of the film.

10. *Girls Trip* (2017): When four college friends head to the Big Easé for the Essence Festival, raunchy madness ensues. As Tiffany Haddish always says, "She readé!"

11. Bonus mention: *Grease 2* (1982): The better of the two *Grease* movies, in our opinion, because the Pink Ladies declare their pledge, "To act cool, to look cool, and to be cool. Till death do us part, THINK PINK!"

Dry

We've been trying to make each other laugh for over twenty years. Lucky for everyone, it seems like we'll be going strong for at least another twenty because with rosé we've found an endless source of material. As discussed in "Rosé 101" (see page 27), there's a spectrum of sweetness with wine, from bone dry to liquid candy. Though we think of ourselves as sweet individuals, there's definitely a touch of 'tude. How we talk is pretty deadpan, and, like the wine we drink, there's not a lot of sugar. Giving this voice to a cheerful pink beverage has been infinitelé hilarious. There is an unlimited number of rosé puns to be made because of the gift that keeps on giving: the French aigu (é) accent. We first used this excellent piece of punctuation on our tote bag, renamed a toté. It has now become a part of our very DNÉ.

The natural home for the aigu has been Instagram, where it graces so many of our captions. Before an Instagram caption is posted to the official Yes Way Rosé account, it has to make us both at least giggle. Laughter is the ultimate barometer, and coming up with rosé jokes has become the best part of our jobs. We love sitting around bouncing jokes off each other like true Instagram comediennes, and over the years we have been able to perfect this highly specialized craft. It's a dirté job that someone has to do, and you best believe there is wine involved.

Since rosé is a fresh wine, we draw inspiration from pop culture to keep the puns coming. Who can predict when Pink, the singer, might step out in pink, the color? Or when a new heartthrob might emerge who just happens to speak French, and both his first and last names rhyme with rosé. Yes Way Timothée Chalamet! Or when Janelle Monáe—Yes Way!—will release a new girl power anthem called "Pynk." There will always be new moments to keep the rosé laughs from running dry.

Elements of Insta-Style

Rosé to the occasion on social media with these photo and caption tips.

Rules for Internet-Breaking Photographé

HIGH-LOW: We value a mash-up both in life and in photos of rosé, favoring shots that have plenty of character. Add an element of charm when showcasing a glorious glass, like with the grilled cheese you're serving alongside it or a trashy magazine.

NO ONE PUTS ROSÉ IN THE CORNER: Keep the focus on the wine. This will make everything else in the frame look better.

NO FILTER NECESSARÉ: Rosé is best photographed in natural light. When you don't need to mess around with filters, you're in a good place. We avoid Instagram filters as much as possible these days and just brighten and sharpen photos a smidge to make them crisp, just like our favorite wines.

THE GRAND SLAM: A glass in front of a pink sunset is a "like" magnet.

How to Aigu

1. When using the l'accent aigu in a caption, pay attention to detail. Choose words that already end with an é. There are great options available for the taking, including *blasé, cliché, risqué, toupée,* and *touché.*

2. Use it in place of words that already end with an "ay" sound, like *sashay* or *chambray*. Alternatively, try adverbs that rhyme imperfectlé. See what we did there?

3. There's more payoff with multisyllabic words. "They say it's your birthdé," for example, reads better than "Happy dé to you."

4. The accent slants down from right to left, people. You have to get this part right!

5. Don't put an é on any old word. Throwing an accent on wine, Mom, sounds like you're saying a glass of rosé is whiny. Hard pass.

This Is How We Do It

A roundup of our greatest Instagram hits reimagined:

A dozen rosés.

Birthdés were the worst days, now we sip rosé when we’re thirsté.

Splish, splash,
rosé in the bath.

Splendor in the glass.

She shoots, she scores.
#swoosh

It's on like rosé pong.

Maybe she's born with it,
maybe it's rosé.

Light as a feather, stiff as a rosé.

Yes Way Snow Day.

Not today, rosé.

ARE
YOU
READÉ
TO
PARTÉ?

Rosé Mixologé

Rosé is a quality ingredient for crafting cocktails, and cocktails are quality ingredients for a fun night. Superb on its own, the wine is also a versatile base for concoctions with a variety of spirits and fresh garnishes. These recipes for mixing pink with the harder stuff range from three-ingredient spritzes to . . . more ambitious offerings. Unleash your inner bartender with our go-to cocktails along with recipes from top mixologists. Start with rosé and you will sip, sip, hooré!

PEROL

Spritz and the City

We liken the Aperol spritz to the "rosé of cocktails": both spritzes and rosé are refreshing, delightful to see, and they go down too easilé. During summer in the city, if you're not nursing a glass of rosé, you are likely to be sipping on a spritz. What happens when you merge these two favorites? Julia Jaksic, the chef and owner of the lovely, pink-accented Cafe Roze in east Nashville, has made mash-up dreams come true with a sparkling rosé riff on a fizzy spritz.

1½ ounces Aperol

2 dashes Angostura Orange Bitters

Dry sparkling rosé

½ orange wheel, for garnish

Pour the Aperol and the orange bitters into a tall Collins glass. Add a large piece of cubed ice to the glass and fill to the top with the rosé. Give the drink a quick stir and garnish with the half orange wheel.

Earth Angel

Will you be mine? The ideal rosé cocktail for Ashley Santoro of the Standard Hotels group incorporates Suze, a French liqueur and a brand of amaro made from gentian root. "It offers a really beautiful herbaceous and bitter element that most don't expect with the combination of rosé," she says. A touch effervescent, this drink is like discovering a secret garden in a glass.

2 ounces rosé

1 ounce Cocchi Americano

½ ounce Suze

½ ounce Aperol

½ ounce lemon juice

½ ounce simple syrup

Soda water

Lemon wheel, for garnish

Pour all ingredients except the soda water and the lemon wheel into a cocktail shaker. Shake, and pour over ice in a rocks glass. Top with the soda water and garnish with the lemon wheel.

Yes Way Sangroné

When we need something harder than rosé, we usually turn to the Negroni. At home we make them in the classic style, with equal parts gin, Campari, and sweet vermouth. For inventive spins on the Italian cocktail, we head to Danté in New York's Greenwich Village, where there's an entire menu dedicated to them. An expert at the craft of the Negroni, Danté's head bartender Stacey Swenson makes a hybrid version with rosé that's inspired by sangria. She says, "I use spirits that are softer on the palate, as this drink, although slightly boozy, is meant to be refreshing and easy drinking."

¾ ounce dry gin (Stacey prefers Botanist Gin)

¾ ounce Aperol or Cappelletti

¾ ounce bianco/blanc vermouth (Stacey recommends Carpano Bianco)

1 teaspoon peach liqueur

3 ounces dry rosé

2 drops orange flower water (optional)

Orange wheel and peach wedges, for garnish

Pinch Maldon Sea Salt Flakes

Fill a large wine glass with ice, combine the first four ingredients, and stir well. Top with the rosé wine and spritz with the orange flower water (if using). Garnish with the orange wheel, peach wedges, and a pinch of Maldon Sea Salt Flakes.

Blame It on the Rosé

This sexy, badass spin on a grapefruit margarita has an unexpectedly edgy element with a rim of black lava salt. Created by a trifecta of boss Chicago mixologists—Diane Corcoran, the beverage director at Three Dots and a Dash; Stephanie Tadd, head bartender at RPM Italian; and Kelly Hanif, head bartender at Hub 51—this is the drink for those who love tequila as much as we do (which is to say, quite a bit).

½ ounce fresh lime juice

½ ounce fresh grapefruit juice

¾ ounce rosé syrup*

½ ounce grapefruit liqueur

1½ ounces blanco tequila

Black lava salt

Grapefruit peel

Dragon fruit, sliced (optional)

Pour all liquid ingredients into a cocktail shaker. Add ice and shake. Strain into a rocks glass over ice. Garnish with a rim of black lava salt and express a grapefruit peel (twisting to release essential oils) over the glass. We like to dress up this cocktail by using the grapefruit peel as a garnish as well as a piece of dragon fruit, simply because it looks cool.

*Rosé syrup: Blend 1 part sugar with 1 part dry rosé wine in a small saucepan over medium heat. Stir until sugar is completely dissolved. Cool and store for multiple drinks.

Summertime Radness

A pretty-in-pink rosé mojito with a hint of aromatic rose is our main squeeze when we crave something with a touch of sweetness. We did not forget the accent here. This calls for rose simple syrup, from the flower. Roses + Rosé = Swoon.

½ lime

1 teaspoon rose simple syrup

6 to 8 fresh mint leaves, with a few small sprigs for garnish

½ cup dry rosé wine

¼ cup club soda

Lime slice, for garnish

Cut the halved lime into wedges, place them in a cocktail shaker with the rose syrup, and muddle to release the lime juice. (*Pro tip:* The back of a spoon works just fine for this if you don't have a muddler.) Add the mint leaves and gently muddle to release the essential oils. Pour in the wine, add ice, and shake the mixture. Strain the contents of the shaker into a Collins glass and top off with a splash of soda water. Rub mint leaves around the rim of the glass, discard, and garnish with more mint sprigs and the lime slice.

Mon Cherré Amour

The fresh, green flavor of basil is a true delight in summertime cocktails, which is why we use it for this pitcher-sized drink that everyone can enjoy. Not too sweet and definitely strong (in a good way), this batch cocktail takes on a lovely ombré color when the bubbles are added. **SERVES 8**

FOR THE CHERRY-BASIL SYRUP:

1 tablespoon black peppercorns

1½ cups (6 ounces) frozen cherries (you can use fresh, but the drink is easier to make with frozen, pitted cherries)

½ cup (3.5 ounces) granulated sugar

½ cup (4 ounces) water

Pinch kosher salt

½ cup fresh basil

MAKES ABOUT 1 CUP In a medium saucepan, toast the peppercorns over medium-high heat until fragrant, about 2 minutes. Add the cherries, sugar, water, and salt and bring to a boil, stirring until the sugar is dissolved. Reduce heat to medium and cook, mashing the berries, until thickened, about 5 minutes. Remove the saucepan from the heat, stir in the basil, and cool to room temperature.

Strain the mixture through a fine-mesh sieve, pressing down to get as much of the berry pulp through as possible. Discard the remaining solids and cool the syrup completely. Use immediately or refrigerate in a closed container for up to 2 weeks.

FOR THE COCKTAILS:

1 recipe cherry-basil syrup
8 ounces gin or vodka

1 bottle (750 milliliters) sparkling rosé, chilled

Ice, for serving

Fresh basil leaves, for garnish

In a pitcher or punch bowl, stir together the syrup and liquor. Right before serving, stir in the sparkling rosé and serve immediately over ice. Garnish with basil leaves. Makes one 30-ounce pitcher.

Yes Way Frosé

We first experimented with the idea of a frosé (also known as a slurpée or slushé) on a girls' trip to Montauk shortly after launching @yeswayrose. We wanted to see if rosé ice cubes in a glass of wine had the same cooling-yet-not-diluting effect as coffee ice cubes in iced coffee. Wow. The experiment exceeded all expectations—we weren't sure if the wine would freeze at all—for chilling the rosé, looking beautiful, and serving as a hilarious activité. Posting our creation on Instagram was a big hit and gave us a glimpse of how enthusiastic people were about the concept of icy rosé. Now we like to think of frosé as the new daiquiri, a drink that summer dreams are made of.

The rosé cube is a no-brainer to make: Pour rosé in an ice cube tray and place in the freezer until hardened. We top our cubes with the same wine used to make them, or make a simple spritz by adding club soda. If you're ready to take your frosé game to the next level, use these brilliant recipes as a guide.

Ice Ice Bébé

At his Los Angeles bar, Block Party, Jason Eisner uses an uber-professional slushé machine to make frosé magic. "If you're balling out and have access to a machine, definitely use it," he says. If, much like us, you don't have a slushé machine lying around, he suggests making this strawberry granita that requires only a blender, a medium-sized baking dish, your freezer, and a fork. Dig in! **SERVES 6**

½ cup sugar

½ cup water

1 pound strawberries, hulled

3 shiso leaves, plus more for garnish (you can substitute mint)

1 bottle (750 milliliters) dry rosé

5 dashes chocolate bitters (don't sleep on this ingredient; it's what takes this frosé to the next level. We use Fee Brothers Aztec Chocolate Bitters made with cacao and spices)

Strawberry, for garnish

Place the sugar, water, strawberries, and shiso leaves in a medium-sized saucepan. Bring to a quick boil, and then reduce the heat and simmer for 10 minutes. Let cool. Put the mixture in a blender and blend on high for 5 to 10 seconds. Strain out the solids and discard.

Pour the strawberry mixture into a shallow baking pan and stir in the wine and bitters. Freeze, stirring every 30 minutes, until the mixture is slush, 5 to 6 hours. Remove from the freezer and stir to break up the larger frozen clumps.

Serve in a Collins glass with a strawberry garnish.

Spring Formal

Sweet, spicy, and bitter at once, this blended frosé from Natasha David, the co-owner of Manhattan's speakeasy-esque cocktail bar Nitecap, checks all the right boxes. **MAKES 1 COCKTAIL**

½ ounce raspberry purée

3 ounces dry rosé wine

1 ounce Cocchi Rosa

1 ounce simple syrup

¼ ounce Amaro Ramazzotti

Fresh mint sprigs, for garnish (optional)

Make the raspberry purée by mixing a handful of raspberries with a small amount of water and blending until smooth. Set aside ½ ounce purée for cocktail, and reserve the remainder for additional cocktails.

Combine all ingredients in a blender with a scoop of ice and blend for about 15 seconds. Pour into a wine glass and garnish with mint sprigs and a fresh raspberry.

Frosémonade Popsicles

These easy-to-make pink lemonade popsicles, spiked with rosé, are the best part about being an adult. **SERVES 16**

1¼ cups (10 ounces) rosé

1¼ cups (10 ounces) water

¾ cup (6 ounces) fresh lemon juice

¾ cup (6 ounces) simple syrup or Yes Way Rosé Simple Syrup (page 167)

1 tablespoon grenadine

1 peach, diced

Combine all ingredients except for the peach in a large bowl. Use a liquid measuring cup to carefully fill popsicle molds about halfway with the mixture. Freeze until just set, about 1 hour. Add a few cubes of peach to each mold (the set layer prevents the peach from sinking to the bottom) and add more of the rosé lemonade mixture—just enough to fill the molds about three-quarters of the way. Insert popsicle sticks and freeze until completely set, about 4 hours. Run the molds under warm running water for a few seconds to loosen the popsicles, then remove and serve. Makes approximately 32 ounces, or 16 popsicles, depending on the mold. Drink any leftovers or use to make ice cubes.

Recipés for a Good Time

Throwing an unforgettable party starts with rosé. The social butterfly of drinks, a beautiful blush glass lights up a room, sparks conversation, and mingles well with food because of its endless versatilité. Draw inspiration from rosé and host the soirée of the year with these menu ideas and pairings that make pink wine's flavors sing. The recipes can be mixed, matched, and built upon for originalité. Just make sure to keep the wine flowing and no one will want to go home earlé.

Yes Way Cheese Tray

The all-time greatest rosé pairing—and our second greatest love—is a well-curated cheese tray. We find an epic spread simplé irresistible and favor a range of cheeses, from mild to stinké, which always includes something blue. One trick to narrow down your choices in the cheese case is to buy based on the rosé you're pairing with, picking cheeses from the same place—or time zone—as the wine you're drinking. A Loire Valley rosé is the perfect choice when cutting into a pyramid-shaped Valençay goat cheese from the same region. Chunks of nutty Parmigiano-Reggiano from Lombardy go especially well with an Italian sparkler made in nearby Franciacorta. These are our tried-and-true favorites, and the supporting cast that puts them over the top.

Cheese Board Faves

Soft goat cheeses and Provence-style rosés are like sisters from different misters, and they get along famously. Try Vermont Creamery's Bonne Bouche, known to us as brain cheese because of the rind's texture, for a tangy option. Or try northern California's Humboldt Fog, with its graphic ribbon of ash down the center, for floral notes, a pleasing crumble when you cut into it, and a cool look on the cheese board.

Manchego is usually the firmest cheese you'll find on our boards. Made with 100 percent sheep's milk, it has a delicate, granular texture and mild flavor that make it a solid choice to appease picky eaters. For braver palates, another option with a similarly dense texture is Midnight Moon. This goat's milk gouda has a slight crunch, a sweet caramel finish, and a name straight out of a fairy tale.

To add an intense, earthy, creamy goodness to the mix, go for either a rich Camembert, Cowgirl Creamery's buttery triple creme from northern

California, or Jasper Hill Farm's oozy and spreadable Harbison from Vermont. These cheeses will melt in your mouth and melt your heart at the same time.

Though it's not everyone's cup of tea (or rosé), we have a weak spot for bold and salty blue cheeses, particularly English Stilton from London's Neals Yard Dairy, as well as strong Roqueforts and Gorgonzolas. Pairing these rich flavors with pink bubbles is sheer decadence.

Pimp out your selection of cheese with the best accoutrements. The cheeses are plenty delicious on their own, but additional flavors turn it up a notch and bring a pop of color to the overall presentation.

Crackers

Let's be real, any cracker is going to be fine for a cheese board. They are really there to serve as vessels to get that delicious cheese off the plate and into your mouth. That said, for our spreads, we are obsessed with a brand of crackers that is aptly named "Toast for Cheese." We discovered these tasty crackers featuring cherries, almonds, and linseeds in a fromagerie in the South of France. Thin and crisp, with just a hint of fruit sugar, they are thankfully available in the United States, too. Barely there rice crackers are another excellent choice for piling on the cheese and help with the goal of not filling up too fast. For added drama in your presentation, try Charcoal Squares from the Fine Cheese Co., which look like goth wheat thins.

Yes Way Charcuteré

Cured meats and cheese are partners in crime. Thinly sliced jamón serrano is a top-notch choice for wrapping around cheese. Dried sausages such as chorizo and soppressata add heat and interest to your board. We tend

to butt heads over the virtues of paté, but the beauty of this kind of spread is that everyone can choose their own adventure.

Fixings

- A drizzle of honéy is essential. On a board, we often opt for fresh honeycomb for show, but we are also obsessed with chili-infused hot honeys.
- Quince paste or fig jams are insanelé delicious spreads to match with stink-forward cheeses.
- Grapes, apple slices, or any kind of fruit adds a fresh quality to the aged components of a cheese board experience.
- Something green and salty such as olives or cornichons makes you feel as though you're eating healthier than you really are—an excellent way to trick yourself into having even more cheese boards in your life.

Sundé Fundé

Spending qualité time catching up with friends over brunch is a treasured Sunday ritual. While double-fisting iced coffées and pink mimosas is no sweat, we always struggle with deciding between sweet and savory food options. To have our (pan)cake and eat it, too, we each get an egg dish—preferably a slow scrambled egg and avocado mash-up—with a sweet plate for the table to share. When we DIY at home, we go for as pink an event as possible with a Yes Way buffet of brunch foods, berries, and beverages, all infused with rosé.

Pink "Bad Ombré" Pancakes

Pancakes are similar to rosé in that the camera loves them and they can be made in a gorgeous array of pinks. Learn the simple trick of mastering an offbeat ombré stack with these super-fluffy buttermilk pancakes—they get their distinctive hues from a few touches of red food coloring. Make your stack extra festive by piling on sliced berries macerated (*keyword alert*) with a little sugar and a splash of rosé. Pour syrup and dollop freshly whipped cream on top—get the shot—and enjoy. If you made too many and want to save for later, these pancakes also freeze incredibly well.

MAKES 16 (5-INCH) PANCAKES

3 cups buttermilk

3 large eggs

8 tablespoons unsalted butter, melted

1 tablespoon pure vanilla extract

3 cups all-purpose flour

¼ cup granulated sugar

2 teaspoons baking powder

2 teaspoons baking soda

1 teaspoon kosher salt

Freeze-dried berries (optional)

Red (liquid) food coloring

Berries, sliced, and whipped cream, for serving

Preheat the oven to 200°F and place a baking sheet inside.

Whisk the buttermilk, eggs, butter, and vanilla together in a medium-sized mixing bowl. In a separate large mixing bowl, whisk together the flour, sugar, baking powder, baking soda, and salt.

Heat a griddle or large nonstick skillet over medium heat. Do not grease!

TIP: Cook the pancakes on low heat to avoid overbrowning—an electric griddle at 250°F to 300°F is best because you can control the temperature and flip multiple pancakes at once.

Add the wet ingredients to the dry ingredients and whisk just to combine. Fold in the freeze-dried berries, if using. Divide the batter into

continues

continued from previous page

three bowls. Pay attention because this is when the rosé gradient magic happens. Add 3 drops of food coloring to one bowl, 2 drops to the second, and 1 drop to the third. Stir each bowl to combine batter with dye. Add more food coloring, 1 drop at a time, to adjust the batter shades to your taste.

Pour one-third cup of batter onto the skillet. When the surface of the pancake is completely covered in bubbles and the edges have set (2 to 3 minutes), flip and cook for 2 to 3 more minutes until set through. Repeat with the remaining batter, keeping the finished pancakes warm in the oven.

Go freestyle with your presentation of the finished pancakes and showcase the stack out of color order to break the ombré mold.

Dress up your stack with whipped cream, fresh berries, and syrup to your liking.

Grapefruit Rosé Mimosa

For a pink take on the brunch classic, use freshly squeezed grapefruit juice in lieu of OJ and top off with pink champs. You can freestyle with the ratio, but we are on the two-thirds rosé to one-third juice team.

Yes Way Parfait

A show-stopping Yes Way parfait is both healthé and a touch boozé when made with poached rhubarb. The tartness of the rhubarb, sweetened with sugar, creates an unexpected kick that complements creamy yogurt nicely. If you're still recovering from last night's parté and aren't in the mood to turn on the oven, this parfait can be whipped up easily with leftover berries from the pancake recipe, no cooking—or rosé—required. **SERVES 6**

2 teaspoons black peppercorns

2 teaspoons green cardamom pods, smashed with the side of a knife

1 cup granulated sugar

1 vanilla bean, split in half, seeds scraped out, pod saved for other use (like flavoring vanilla sugar)

2 cups dry rosé

Pinch kosher salt

10 to 12 stalks (1 pound) rhubarb, cut into 3-inch pieces

4½ cups labneh or Greek yogurt (¾ cup per person)

Granola, for topping (our numero uno choice is by the granola queen Elizabeth Stein of Purely Elizabeth, who is a dear childhood friend)

Line a baking sheet with parchment paper.

Toast the peppercorns and cardamom in a large skillet over medium heat until fragrant, about 2 minutes. Add the sugar, vanilla, rosé, and salt and bring to a simmer over medium-high heat. Stir until the sugar is dissolved, then continue simmering until the mixture is syrupy, 3 to 6 minutes.

Add the rhubarb and simmer, turning once halfway through cooking, until the rhubarb is tender but not falling apart, about 3 minutes. With a slotted spatula, carefully transfer the rhubarb to the prepared baking sheet and cool to room temperature.

Continue cooking the syrup until reduced to ½ cup, 3 to 6 minutes more. Strain and discard solids. Top rhubarb with the syrup.

Layer the labneh or Greek yogurt with the poached rhubarb and granola in a glass. Use stemless wine glasses for serving or arrange everything in a bowl and grab a spoon.

Ladiés Night

Don't hold back when it comes to an all-pink-everything dinner parté—it's a winning theme for a bridal shower, bachelorette extravaganza, or highly elevated meeting with your book club. Take the pressure off the evening and delegate so that it's a team effort, with each friend bringing a different pink-tinted course. We call being on wine duty! The devil is in the details, so go matché matché with the dress code, flowers, and the wine, too. To perfectly pair this menu, we consulted with one of the funniest women we know, the wine guru and host of the Whitney A. Channel, Whitney Adams. Oh girls, they wanna have rosé!

Yes Way Canapés

Create a hat trick of yummy bite-size canapés in an assortment of pretty pinks.

For a wine that pairs with all three, Whitney suggests sparkling. *"Pink bubbles are my go-to for anything 'appetizer.' An elegant Cava Rosado or Crémant de Bourgogne will be best friends with a wide variety of bites, from tartare to salty feta."*

Tuna Tartare Crisps

SERVES 6
PREPARE JUST BEFORE SERVING

12 ounces sushi-grade tuna, raw

1 large shallot, minced (¼ cup)

¼ cup Champagne vinegar

¼ cup avocado or walnut oil

2 limes, juice and zest, finely grated

1 teaspoon pink peppercorns, plus more for garnish, smashed with the side of a knife

¼ cup basil leaves, thinly sliced (chiffonade)

Kosher salt and freshly ground black pepper

Endive leaves, for serving (optional)

Freeze the tuna for 15 minutes to make cutting easier, and place a metal mixing bowl in the refrigerator. Remove the tuna from freezer and, with a very sharp knife, cut it into ¼-inch cubes and place in the chilled bowl.

Whisk the shallot, vinegar, oil, lime juice and zest, and peppercorns in a small bowl.

Pour the vinaigrette over the tuna. Add the basil and fold together just to combine. Taste and adjust seasoning with salt and pepper.

Plate the portions individually using a ring mold or biscuit cutter to shape them neatly. Alternatively, scoop the tartare into endive leaves for sophisticated finger food.

PB + F (Prosciutto, Butter, and Fig)

Make sure to splurge on imported prosciutto and go for the best bread and butter possible when preparing this delicious bite. **SERVES 6**

1 loaf raisin-walnut bread, sliced and toasted

Butter, slightly softened

½ pound prosciutto

6 ripe figs, stems trimmed and quartered lengthwise

Maldon salt and freshly ground black pepper

Generously spread each slice of bread with butter. Top with prosciutto and figs. Sprinkle with flaky Maldon salt and pepper. Serve.

Watermelon + Whipped Feta Bites

SERVES 6
(WHIPPED FETA MAKES ABOUT 1 CUP)

8 ounces feta cheese

8 ounces Greek yogurt

1 teaspoon lemon zest

2 tablespoons extra-virgin olive oil, divided

¼ large seedless watermelon, flesh cut into 2-inch batons

Juice of 1 lemon

Maldon salt and freshly ground black pepper

Aleppo-style pepper or red pepper flakes, for serving

Pulse the cheese, yogurt, lemon zest, and 1 tablespoon oil in a food processor until smooth. Transfer to a small serving bowl.

Cut the watermelon into batons, leaving the rind on. Squeeze the lemon over the watermelon and drizzle with 1 tablespoon extra-virgin olive oil. Season with Maldon salt and freshly ground pepper. Sprinkle with the Aleppo-style pepper or red pepper flakes before serving. Present the melon crudité-style with the whipped feta on the side.

Shine Bright Like a Beet Risotto

The Rihanna of risottos, this earthy rendition, with its vibrant hue, brings the intensité. **SERVES 6 (SMALL/SIDE DISH PORTIONS)**

3 tablespoons olive oil

1 yellow onion, finely chopped (1 cup)

2 large red beets (about 1 pound), peeled and shredded on the large holes of a box grater

1½ cups arborio rice

Kosher salt and freshly ground black pepper

1 cup dry rosé wine

6 cups chicken broth, warm

1 cup (4 ounces) Parmesan cheese, grated, plus more for serving

1 tablespoon fresh horseradish, finely grated, plus more for serving (prepared horseradish can be substituted)

1 lemon, zest, finely grated, and juice

Fresh dill sprigs,for garnish

Heat the oil over medium-high heat in a Dutch oven or large sauté pan. Add the onion and beets and cook, stirring, until softened, about 10 minutes. Add the rice, 1½ teaspoons salt, and ½ teaspoon pepper and stir to combine.

Lower heat to medium, add the wine, and cook, stirring frequently, until the liquid is fully absorbed. Repeat the process with the broth, adding ¾ cup at a time, or until the rice is tender and coated in a velvety sauce. If the rice is too firm or dry, continue cooking, adding water ½ cup at a time until the correct consistency is achieved.

Remove the rice from the heat and stir in the cheese, horseradish, and lemon zest and lemon juice. Adjust seasoning and serve immediately, garnishing with Parmesan, horseradish, and dill.

Slow-Roasted Salmon with Olive-Crouton Vinaigrette

Salmon is a natural choice for your party's entrée because the color is frequently used to describe rosé. This Mediterranean-influenced recipe is prepared with a variety of greens to complement the fish and its pale shade of pink.

"Don't overlook lesser-known regions or styles for this dinner!" Whitney says. *"Venture out of your rosé comfort zone and try something new. With the Mediterranean flavors of the salmon, and beet risotto's subtle earthiness, dive into more mineral and robust rosés, like hearty, and sometimes aged Spanish rosados from Rioja and Ribera del Duero, or cherry-licious and slightly bitter Italian Chiaretto rosé that will prove a nice departure from the norm."*

FOR THE SALMON:

6 (6-ounce) salmon fillets or a side of salmon

Olive or avocado oil

Kosher salt and freshly ground black pepper

5 tablespoons olive or avocado oil, divided

5 slices rustic bread, cut into ¾-inch cubes (about 6 cups)

Allow the salmon to sit at room temperature for 30 minutes prior to cooking.

Adjust rack to the middle position in your oven and preheat to 275°F. Line a rimmed baking sheet with parchment paper. Drizzle the salmon with oil and gently rub to evenly coat. Place the salmon skin-side down on the prepared baking sheet and season with salt and pepper. Cook for 15 to 20 minutes. When fully cooked the salmon will look translucent and may appear as though it's not done—don't worry, it is. You're aiming for a nice medium-rare fish here.

While the fish is baking, heat 2 tablespoons oil in a large skillet over medium-high heat until shimmering. Add the bread and cook, stirring occasionally, until golden, about 5 minutes. Transfer to a large mixing bowl.

continues

continued from previous page

4 teaspoons Dijon mustard

¼ cup white wine vinegar

1 cup parsley, coarsely chopped

1 cup (6 ounces) Castelvetrano olives, pitted and coarsely chopped

½ cup raw pistachios, coarsely chopped

1 tablespoon capers, rinsed and drained

Mixed greens, for serving, seasoned with salt and pepper

FOR THE OLIVE-CROUTON VINAIGRETTE:

In a small mixing bowl, whisk together the mustard, vinegar, and 3 tablespoons of oil until combined.

Add the parsley, olives, pistachios, and capers to the croutons and stir. Drizzle in half of the vinaigrette.

Serve the salmon with the croutons and mixed greens, drizzled with the remaining vinaigrette if desired.

Yes Way Ovenlé Rosewater Vanilla Cake

When we met Agatha Kulaga and Erin Patinkin, the owners of New York's beloved and rapidly growing bakery Ovenly, we immediately hit it off. It was clear these work wives have a strong vision for their business and an affection for each other, which come through in each of their delectable treats. We knew they would be our friends for life the first night we hung out, when we crushed cans of rosé and they agreed to make our pink dessert dream come true.

The velvety vanilla cake they concocted is infused with rosé and rosewater and topped off with a rosé buttercream icing. Re-creating this will definitely take effort and time, so enlist your bestie as sous chef and make it half the work, double the fun.

"Most people run from sweet rosé and drink dry only, but when made well and with the right balance of acidity, off-dry rosé is a beautiful thing. The naturally sparkling rosés from the Bugey appellation in France are so freaking pretty and delicious I dare anyone to dislike them. Look to producers Renardat Fache or Patrick Bottex for the gold standards." **MAKES ONE DOUBLE-LAYER 9-INCH CAKE**

Unsalted butter, softened, and all-purpose flour, for preparing cake pans

4 cups cake flour, sifted

2 tablespoons baking powder

1 teaspoon salt

1½ cups heavy cream, at room temperature

1 cup full-fat sour cream, at room temperature

1 pound butter (16 ounces, 4 sticks), softened

2½ cups sugar

6 large eggs, at room temperature

2 tablespoons vanilla extract

2 tablespoons rosewater

Preheat the oven to 350°F. Grease two 9-inch cake pans with butter and dust with flour. Line with parchment rounds and grease the rounds.

In a large bowl, whisk together the cake flour, baking powder, and salt. Set aside.

In a medium bowl, whisk together the heavy cream and sour cream. Set aside.

In the bowl of a stand mixer fitted with a paddle attachment (or using a hand-held mixer), cream the butter and sugar together until light and fluffy, on medium speed, for about 3 minutes. Add the eggs to the butter mixture, one at a time, turning off the machine to scrape down the sides of the bowl with a rubber spatula after each addition. Add the vanilla and rosewater and mix for another minute until the mixture is well combined and smooth.

With the machine off, add a third of the flour mixture to the mixing bowl. Mix on low until the flour mixture is just incorporated. Add half of the sour cream mixture, and beat on medium-low until just incorporated. Add another third of the flour mixture, and repeat the process, finishing with the remaining third of the flour mixture.

When all the ingredients have been added and appear almost combined, stop the mixer. Using a spatula, stir the batter and incorporate any remaining dry flour. Do not overmix.

Divide the batter equally between the prepared cake pans. Bake for 30 to 35 minutes, or until a toothpick inserted in the center of the cake comes out clean.

While the cake layers are baking, prepare the Yes Way Rosé Simple Syrup (recipe on page 167).

Let the cakes cool on wire racks for 20 minutes before turning them out of the pans, and then let them cool completely.

Once the cake layers have cooled, use a toothpick or fork to poke some small holes in the tops of each cake layer.

continues

continued from page 164

Brush the simple syrup generously over cake layers and let it soak in.

Assemble and frost the cake with Rosé Buttercream (recipe below). Using a serrated knife, level the cake layers if needed. At this point, we like to wrap the layers and freeze them for at least an hour, which makes it easier to frost the cake without doing a preliminary layer of frosting, known as a crumb coat. Once frozen, using an offset spatula or wide flat knife, spread buttercream filling over the bottom layer, aiming for a ½-inch-thick coating. Stack the next cake layer directly on top of the first. Spread the remaining buttercream over the top layer and sides of the cake. Even out the top and sides and decorate with dried rose petals.

ROSÉ BUTTERCREAM

2 cups dry rosé (we highly recommend our own Yes Way Rosé for this recipe)

16 tablespoons (1 cup, 8 ounces) unsalted butter, cold

7 cups confectioners' sugar, divided, plus more for thickening

¼ to ½ cup heavy cream

3 to 4 drops pink or red food coloring (preferably all natural)

Dried rose buds or petals, for decoration

In a small saucepan over medium heat, bring the rosé to a simmer. Cook until syrupy and reduced to about ½ cup, about 20 to 25 minutes. Set aside to cool completely.

Cut the cold butter into ½-inch pieces. Let it come to room temperature.

In the bowl of a stand mixer fitted with a paddle attachment, combine the butter, 3 cups of confectioners' sugar, and ¼ cup heavy cream, and mix on low until just incorporated. Then beat on medium-high until the mixture is creamy and ingredients are incorporated, about 1 minute. Scrape down the bowl with a rubber spatula.

Add ½ cup of the rosé reduction to the buttercream and mix on low until fully incorporated. Using a spatula, scrape down the sides of the bowl to incorporate any remaining rosé.

Add more confectioners' sugar, 1 cup at a time, and mix on low until the buttercream is thick but spreadable. Beat for 1 minute after each addition. Once you have your desired consistency, scrape down the sides of the bowl.

Add the food coloring (or coat a toothpick with pink or red gel coloring) and mix into the buttercream, which should take on a light pink color.

Raise the speed to medium-high and beat for 3 to 4 minutes, until very light and fluffy. If it is too thick, add a little more cream. If too thin, add a little more confectioners' sugar. Add more coloring, as needed, to reach a light pink color, and beat buttercream until desired color is reached.

YES WAY ROSÉ SIMPLE SYRUP

½ cup sugar

½ cup dry rosé

3 tablespoons rosewater

In a small saucepan, bring the sugar, rosé, and rosewater to a boil.

Simmer until the sugar is dissolved, about 3 minutes.

Remove from the heat and let cool completely. Store syrup in a glass jar and save for up to 1 month.

Mastering the Art of French Drinking: A Julia-Inspired Dinner Parté

A trailblazing woman who had a special joie de vivre, Julia Child is a huge hero of ours. We feel connected to her love of food, butter, and the fact that she only started cooking seriously in her early thirties, which happens to be when we began pursuing our passion for rosé. On a recent trip to Provence, we were incredibly fortunate to stay next door to La Pitchoune, the tiny countryside house she built with her husband in the 1960s, where she entertained legendary foodie friends like James Beard and M. F. K. Fisher. This menu pays homage to Ms. Child's joyful spirit and that spectacular trip. As Julia said—she had a memorable line for everything—*"Life itself is the proper binge."* We agree wholeheartedlé.

WWJCD, or What Would Julia Child Drink?

Julia's signature aperitif was the upside-down martini, which is 2 parts vermouth to 1 part gin, instead of the other way around. Rosé-ify this drink by using a rosé vermouth or Lillet.

Domaine Tempier
BANDOL
Appellation Bandol contrôlée
2016
KERMIT LYNCH WINE MERCHANT

Roast Chicken with Shallots + Potatoes

"The best way to execute French cooking is to get good and loaded and whack the hell out of a chicken. Bon appétit." —Julia Child

If there was ever an occasion to break out a special rosé, it's for this dinner. Open a 1-year or even 2-year aged bottle of Domaine Tempier Bandol and channel Julia's esteemed crew. **SERVES 4**

Olive oil

1 (3½- to 4-pound) chicken

Kosher salt and freshly ground black pepper

1 teaspoon Herbes de Provence

1 head of garlic, whole, cut in half crosswise

1 lemon, washed and cut in half

12 large shallots (about 1½ pounds), peeled and cut in half lengthwise

8 Red Bliss potatoes (about 2 pounds), scrubbed and halved

TIP: Use about ¾ teaspoon salt per pound to perfectlé season chicken. Check the package for weight and multiply by 0.75.

Adjust oven rack to the middle position and preheat oven to 425°F. Line a rimmed baking sheet with foil (a cleanup hack!) or have a roasting pan handy. Drizzle the sheet or pan with oil.

Remove the bag, if any, from the chicken's cavity and store for another use (like gravy) or discard. Rinse the chicken inside and out under cold running water, then thoroughly pat dry with paper towels.

Carefully run your fingers in between the skin and flesh to loosen it. Combine the salt, pepper, and Herbes de Provence and rub under and over the skin. Stuff the chicken's cavity with the garlic and lemon. Tie the legs together with kitchen twine and tuck the wing tips under the chicken.

Place the chicken on the prepared sheet or pan. Arrange the shallots and potatoes around the chicken, drizzle the vegetables with olive oil, and season with salt and pepper.

Roast for 60 to 75 minutes, or until an instant-read thermometer reads 160°F from the thigh. The juices will run clear when it's done. Remove from the oven and let it rest for 10 minutes before carving. Serve with the shallots and potatoes.

Pan-Roasted Haricots Verts with Pine Nuts

"You don't have to cook fancy or complicated masterpieces—just good food from fresh ingredients." —Julia Child **SERVES 6**

2 tablespoons pine nuts

2 tablespoons unsalted butter

1 pound haricots verts, trimmed

Kosher salt and freshly ground black pepper

1 lemon, zest, finely grated, and juice

Place the pine nuts in a large skillet and cook over medium heat, shaking the pan occasionally, until golden, 3 to 5 minutes. Transfer to a bowl.

Melt the butter in the same skillet, now empty, over medium-high heat. Add the haricots verts and ¼ cup of water, and season with salt and pepper. Cover and cook until the beans are crisp and bright green, about 3 minutes. Remove the lid and continue cooking until crisp-tender and browned in spots, 3 to 5 minutes longer. Add the pine nuts and the lemon zest and juice, and toss to combine.

BANDOL
2016

Cauliflower Gratin

"If you're afraid of butter, use cream." —Julia Child **SERVES 4 TO 6**

2 cups whole milk

1 small yellow onion, peeled and cut in half

2 garlic cloves, peeled and smashed

1 bay leaf

1 small bunch thyme

1 large head green or white cauliflower (about 2½ pounds), cut into large florets

Kosher salt and freshly ground black pepper

2 tablespoons unsalted butter

2 tablespoons all-purpose flour

Pinch of freshly grated nutmeg

2 cups (8 ounces) grated Gruyere cheese, divided

Preheat the oven to 425°F (if not already making the chicken).

Place the milk, onion, garlic, bay leaf, and thyme in a small saucepan and bring to a boil over medium-high heat. Remove from the heat and allow the milk to steep for 20 minutes. Remove and discard aromatics.

Bring a medium pot of water to a boil. Add 1 tablespoon salt and the cauliflower florets and cook until florets are just tender, 4 to 5 minutes. Drain and leave in colander while you prepare the sauce.

Melt the butter in a medium saucepan over medium heat. Whisk in the flour and cook, whisking constantly for 2 minutes. Pour in the warm milk and continue whisking to avoid lumps. Cook until thickened, about 2 minutes. Remove from heat and stir in half of the cheese, ½ teaspoon salt, ½ teaspoon pepper, and nutmeg. Taste and adjust seasoning.

Place the cauliflower in an 8 × 8-inch or other medium baking dish. Pour the sauce in and stir to combine. Sprinkle the remaining cheese over the top. Place on middle rack in oven while you attend to the chicken. Bake until sauce is bubbling and top is browned, about 15 minutes.

Rosemaré-Honey Crème Brûlée

"I think every woman should have a blowtorch." —Julia Child

We recommend a fancé French Champagne like La Caravelle Rosé with dessert. It's sophisticated while relatively affordable—as far as Champagnes go—and is made by one of our women-in-wine obsessions Rita Jammet and her husband, André. **SERVES 6**

SPECIAL EQUIPMENT:

6 (6-ounce capacity) ramekins

Pastry torch: It may seem serious, but torches are inexpensive, available online, and you can handle it!

3 cups heavy cream

¾ cup amber honey (use whatever honey you have on hand, but a darker variety will provide a bolder and more defined flavor)

½ teaspoon kosher salt

3 large sprigs fresh rosemary

6 large egg yolks, at room temperature

½ cup granulated sugar

Adjust an oven rack to the middle position (remove any racks above that) and preheat the oven to 325°F. Bring a kettle or a medium saucepan of water to a boil and remove from heat. Place a tea towel in a roasting pan or 9 x 13-inch baking pan. You'll use this setup for a water bath, or bain-marie, which is what will cook your crème brûlée gently.

Stir the cream, honey, and salt together in a medium saucepan. Add the rosemary and bring to a simmer over medium heat. Remove from heat, cover, and allow flavors to meld for 30 minutes. Remove and discard rosemary. If the cream has gotten cold, quickly rewarm and transfer it to a liquid measuring cup or another vessel with a spout.

To make whisking easier, make an anchor for your mixing bowl by dampening a tea towel, rolling it up, and shaping it into a nest. Place a large bowl in the nest and whisk the egg yolks until smooth.

Slowly whisk a small amount of the warm cream into the yolks to temper them, then whisk in the rest. Strain the mixture back into the liquid measuring cup. Skim off and discard any foam.

continues

continued from page 175

Arrange the ramekins in the prepared roasting pan. Divide the mixture evenly among the ramekins. Carefully place the pan on the oven rack and pour in enough hot water to reach halfway up the sides of the ramekins.

Bake the custards until the tops set but there's still some jiggle in the center, 30 to 60 minutes, depending on the height of the ramekins. Very carefully transfer the entire pan to the cooktop surface or a large cooling rack. With the help of a spatula and a dry tea towel, carefully lift each ramekin out and onto a cooling rack. Allow to come to room temperature, then refrigerate, uncovered, for at least 1 hour and up to 2 days.

Sprinkle the sugar on the surface of the custards. With a pastry torch, apply the flame to the sugared tops until it bubbles and caramelizes. Cool to allow the caramel to harden and then serve.

Backyard Bash

When it's summertime and the livin's easé, every type of al fresco dining calls for rosé. Outdoors is, after all, a rosé's natural habitat. If you're firing up the grill in the backyard or hosting a rooftop barbecue, bigger is better when choosing a bottle. A supersized magnum offers an almost never-ending supply of wine and adds a beautiful pink touch to the decor. You could also get creative and pour out the whole bottle as a base for rosé sangria or punch (see page 119). Be sure not to forget outdoor speakers and a playlist. With friends and family around, Fleetwood Mac blasting, and a sweaty glass in hand, any place can feel like a sunny paradise.

S'mores

Grab a stick and kick it back to the days of summer camp with s'mores over a fire. Simply combine graham crackers, toasted marshmallows, and chocolate in a delicious sandwich for dessert perfection. Put a rosé spin on this sweet treat by using cute pink marshmallows and, if you're feeling crazé, a cut-up Snickers or Kit-Kat in place of plain milk chocolate. When building a fire is not an option—perhaps it's not the best idea on a rooftop—you can roast the marshmallows over embers in the grill.

Yes Way Crudités

Eat your greens while drinking your pinks! Arrange a monochromatic crudités tray with crunchy snap peas, cucumber wedges, asparagus, and celery sticks for a stylish take on the veggie platter. Add a creamy Green Goddess dressing for dipping (store-bought is just fine—it will be our secret!), which hits the spot while adding to the color theme.

Pro tip: Visit the local farmers' market and pick fresh summer vegetables that will taste and look better than the prepackaged supermarket varieté.

Yes Way Ceviché

Served chilled, like rosé, ceviché is a quick and eye-catching appetizer that packs a lot of punch. **SERVES 6**

1 pound fresh ocean fish (skinless) fillets, such as red snapper

2 large pink grapefruits

2 limes, zest, finely grated, and juice (about 2 tablespoons juice)

1 red onion, thinly sliced (about 1 cup)

1 garlic clove, minced

1 Serrano chili, ribs and seeds removed, minced

1 tablespoon ketchup

2 teaspoons Worcestershire sauce

1 cup cilantro leaves (optional)

Kosher salt and freshly ground pepper

Tortilla chips or warm tortillas, for serving

Chill the fish and a medium mixing bowl in the freezer for 10 minutes.

Cut off the top and bottom of the grapefruit; you should see the flesh. Set the grapefruit on a cutting board. Using downward strokes, slice the peel off. Again, you should see the flesh. Trim off any white bits of pith. With a paring knife, remove each segment by carefully cutting between the membranes, and place the segments in the chilled bowl. Squeeze in the juice of the remaining grapefruit (about 1 cup). Stir in the lime zest and juice, onion, garlic, chili, ketchup, and Worcestershire sauce.

With a very sharp knife, cut the fish into ¼-inch-thick slices. Add the fish and cilantro to the grapefruit mixture and gently fold. Allow to sit for 10 minutes, just until the fish edges begin to turn opaque.

NOTE: You can let the fish marinate for up to 30 minutes, but the longer it sits, the mushier it will become.

Taste and adjust seasoning with salt and pepper. Serve immediately with tortilla chips or warm tortillas.

Grilled Steak and Corn Salad

For a classic steak on the grill, we opt for a New York strip or rib eye cooked medium rare, aka rosé rare, so it's just the right shade of pink. Slice and serve alongside a vibrant summer corn salad with mozzarella for the backyard meal of champions. **SERVES 6**

3 tablespoons red wine vinegar

2 teaspoons Dijon mustard

¼ cup extra-virgin olive oil

Kosher salt and freshly ground black pepper

6 ears fresh corn

2 cups grape tomatoes, halved

8 ounces fresh mozzarella, torn into bite-sized pieces

6 scallions, thinly sliced

1 cup fresh parsley, chopped

1 cup basil leaves, chopped

FOR THE STEAK:

TIP: Every grill is different, and cooking time will vary based on the size and cut of the meat.

As a general guideline: Get steaks that are about 1½ inches thick. Let the steaks sit at room temperature for 30 minutes. Clean and oil the grill while you are waiting. Season both sides of the meat generously with kosher salt and freshly ground pepper. Grill steaks, flipping occasionally and testing temperature with a probe thermometer. Cook steaks 12 to 15 minutes for medium rare (125°F to 130°F internal temperature).

Transfer the meat to a cutting board and rest for 5 to 10 minutes before serving.

FOR THE SALAD:

Whisk the vinegar and mustard together in a small bowl. Whisk in the olive oil and season with salt and pepper.

Cut the kernels off the corn over a large bowl (you should have about 4 cups). You can also grill the corn before doing this. Add the remaining ingredients, season with salt and pepper, and toss to combine. Whisk the dressing to recombine and drizzle over the salad.

THANK YOU
A rosé a day keeps the bad vibes away.

Couch Parté

Staying in with a TV dinner becomes a prime opportunité for delicious comfort food pairings when home is where the rosé is. What's on the menu and where it comes from depend on how lazy you're feeling. For an Oscar party, big game night, or reality show binge, mix home-cooked food with deliveré so you can lounge on the couch and sip on something pink while waiting for the food to arrive. With rosé in the fridge, you can be the hostess with the mostess, even in sweatpants.

Yes Way Deliveré

Sometimes you just cannot bring yourself to cook and instead surrender to the ease of takeout. For those nights keep the chic factor alive by popping a bottle of bubblé. The refreshing fizz of sparkling wine complements strong, spicy flavors and balances both sweet and sour. Serve crisp bubbles with cold, spicy sesamé noodles, Szechuan string beans with chili, or Kung Pao chicken to accentuate their scrumptiousness. Rosé lovers of the world, spice up your life!

Pizza

When the moon hits your eye like a big pizza pie, that's a rosé! Pairing a quintessential NYC-style pie with classic Provençal rosé is our definition of living your best life.

Old Baé Crab Mac + Cheese

We grew up in Baltimore, where the ultimate summer pastime is feasting on messy Old Bay–seasoned Maryland crabs around a brown paper–covered picnic table. This is typically a beer-and-bib kind of situation, but we've learned rosé works just as well. To get the taste of this coastal treat at home, and in a tidier fashion, make lump crab mac and cheese. The crunchy Old Bay topping in this recipe includes another YWR favorite: *chips.* For bonus points, use Utz crab-flavored potato chips, a Charm Cité gem. **SERVES 8**

4 cups coarse bread crumbs (from 4 slices of bread if making your own, or use prepackaged Panko style)

NOTE: You can substitute half of the bread crumbs with 2 cups of crushed potato chips. We do.

6 tablespoons butter, melted

1 tablespoon Old Bay

FOR THE CRUMB TOPPING:

Combine all ingredients in a medium mixing bowl and set aside.

continues

continued from previous page

FOR THE MAC AND CHEESE:

1 pound corkscrew pasta

6 tablespoons unsalted butter, divided

1 yellow onion, finely chopped (1 cup)

2 garlic cloves, finely chopped

1 pound lump crab meat, drained and patted dry

1 lemon, zest, finely grated, and juice

¼ cup all-purpose flour

1 tablespoon dry mustard

4 cups whole milk, warm

1 pound sharp cheddar cheese, grated (4 cups)

¼ cup thinly sliced chives (optional)

Adjust an oven rack to the top third position and preheat the oven to 425°F.

Bring a large pot of water and 1 tablespoon salt to a boil over high heat. Add the pasta and cook until al dente (see package instructions). Reserve 1 cup of cooking water and drain.

While the pasta is cooking, melt 2 tablespoons of the butter over medium-high heat in a large Dutch oven. Add the onion and cook, stirring, until softened, about 5 minutes. Add the garlic and cook until fragrant, 1 minute. Add the crab, season with salt and pepper, and cook until warmed through, about 3 minutes. Transfer crab into a bowl and stir in lemon zest and juice.

Lower heat to medium and melt the remaining 4 tablespoons butter in the now-empty Dutch oven. Whisk in the flour and dry mustard and cook, whisking constantly for 2 minutes. Slowly pour in the warm milk, whisking constantly to avoid lumps. Cook until thickened, about 2 minutes. Remove from heat and stir in the cheese. Taste and adjust seasoning.

Add the pasta to the sauce and stir to combine. Stir in the crab and (optional) chives. You can transfer the mixture to a 13 × 9-inch baking dish or leave it in the Dutch oven. Top with the bread-crumb mixture and bake until golden brown, about 15 minutes. Serve immediately.

Birthdé Cake Crispies

This colorful take on the cupboard classic was created by our hometown hero Krystal Mack, a Baltimore baker and the owner of BLK//SUGAR, a culinary art and lifestyle concept. It's a bright and playful dessert option that—of course—tastes amazing with rosé! **MAKES ABOUT 20 SQUARES**

3 tablespoons butter

1 (10-ounce) package marshmallows

2 teaspoons vanilla bean paste or 2 teaspoons pure vanilla extract (Krystal recommends McCormick's Pure Vanilla)

6 cups (6 ounces) of crispy rice cereal

2 to 4 teaspoons rainbow sprinkles

Coat a 13 × 9-inch baking pan with cooking spray. In a large pot, melt the butter over low heat. Add the marshmallows and stir until completely melted. Remove from heat. Add the vanilla bean paste or vanilla extract and stir until well combined. Pour in the cereal and sprinkles and stir until well coated with the marshmallow mixture. Using a rubber spatula, press the mixture into the prepared pan. Cool. Cut. Enjoy.

ROSÉ ASTROLOGÉ

When Mercuré is in retrograde or Mars is energizing your seventh house, there's a rosé written in the stars for you. Consult these horoscopes to find out which style is most compatible with your celestial personalité.

Aries

March 21–April 20

With your daredevil spirit and dynamic courage, you, high-energy Aries, could benefit from chilling out and sipping a bottle of spritzy, refreshing pink Txakoli from Spain's Basque country. The teensy bubbles and effervescence won't dull your fire but might give you a moment of Yes Way Namasté.

Taurus

April 21–May 21

Taurus, you are a study in contrasts: Generous, warm-hearted, and financially responsible, you also have a bit of an indulgent and lazy side. Offering great value and the same volume as four regular wine bottles, a quaffable box of rosé might be your perfect match. The box offers plenty for your personal consumption and plenty to share, with an easy-to-use tap that requires minimal effort when it's time for refills.

Gemini

May 22–June 21

Your curiosity and versatility, smart and lively Gemini, make you the ideal candidate for an intellectual, hard-to-pronounce rosé from Central and Eastern Europe. The stories in the bottles from Hungary, Slovenia, and Croatia are just waiting to be told, and you, the great communicator, are the one to drink and tell them. Put your investigative skills to work and track down a Kékfrankos rosé from Hungarian winemaker Tamás Dúzsi.

Cancer

June 22–July 22

Imaginative, emotional, faithful Cancer, as a cautious skeptic who can sometimes be a bit tenacious, you should find yourself a dependable favorite that will never let you down. Select a classic peachy Provençal rosé and stick with it. Shops often offer case discounts, so you can stock up. Reliability is a good thing, and if you find it in your wine, it might take some pressure off your wallet and your friends. We suggest BY OTT by Domaine Ott, Aix Rosé, or Yes Way Rosé, obviouslé!

Leo

July 23–August 21

Lionhearted Leo, you are loving, enthusiastic, and wildly creative, but not without a bossy edge. A fiery sign that thrives in the spotlight, Leo is certainly the queen of the jungle. You deserve Grand Cru Rosé Champagne: ebullient, regal, and expensive. We may never be royals, but that shouldn't stop us from living like one.

Virgo

August 22–September 23

Practical, meticulous, and feminine, just like some of the best rosés out there, you're a tough critic, Virgo—some might even call you a perfectionist. Find yourself a terroir-driven rosé made from Cabernet Franc—as simultaneously earthy and put-together as you are—perhaps from the winery of the venerable Olga Raffault in Chinon. Your analytical self will enjoy tasting (and judging) as many rosés as possible to see how they measure up.

Libra

September 24–October 23

Do you find it hard to make choices and change your mind often? It's not your fault, dear Libra, it comes with the territoré. Thankfully, so does being charming, romantic, and easygoing. Find the well-balanced bottle you crave by enlisting the help of a sommelier or trusted neighborhood wine shop. They can help you through the difficult decision-making process when it comes to choosing a bottle, tipping the rosé scales in your favor. For a reliable go-to, try an elegant people pleaser such as Costaripa Rosamara from Italy's Veneto region.

Scorpio

October 24–November 22

People are drawn to passionate, exciting, strong-willed Scorpio's magnetic personalité, much like a brightly hued Garnacha-driven rosado from Rioja. Packing a vibrant punch, these persuasive pink powerhouses are the life of the party, just like you. Go against your secretive nature and share this tip—and wine—with all of your pink-loving friends.

Sagittarius

November 23–December 22

Upbeat and adventurous Sagittarians live and die by the belief that "all good things are wild and free," so funky pink bubbles made in the *pét-nat* style are the pick for you. Each one is a little different—it's kind of alive, after all—and you'll enjoy the journé. Your blind optimism and sense of humor come in handy when you occasionally pop a bottle that's a little too weird.

Capricorn

December 23–January 20

You, Ram, are a cool, calm, and confident climber, with the ambition and discipline to reach great heights. Explore high-altitude rosés from the soaring peaks of the Argentinian Andes (Wölffer Estate's Finca from Mendoza is a nice choice) or the snowcapped Austrian Alps (we're into Pratsch rosé). It's never lonely at the top if you have rosé.

Aquarius

January 21–February 19

Natural wines, those made with little-to-no additives, are friendly, forward-thinking, and eccentric, just like water-bearing Aquarius. Since you are both a humanitarian and an extremist, the ethical aspects of natural winemaking appeal to you as much as the cultural zeitgeist that surrounds some of the trendier bottles. Track down an unusual and wonderful Susucaru Rosato from Sicily's Frank Cornelissen for full effect.

Pisces

February 20–March 20

Visionary Pisces, set your intuitive sights on the New World and explore the varied rosés of sunny California. Creative winemakers are experimenting with all sorts of interesting things, from growing uncommon European grape varieties like Trousseau and Dolcetto, to vinifying their wines in egg-shaped concrete containers that resemble a space shuttle. Your open-mindedness and idealism are all that's needed.

Parlez-Vous Rosé? A Yes Way Glossaré

BROSÉ: A beer-guzzling gentleman who has gone to the pink side.

BUBBLÉ: Rosé plus bubbles. A pink sparkling wine that, when popped, gets the parté started.

BYOR: Bring Your Own Rosé. This is a chance to impress friends and admirers by showing off your rosé prowess at a gathering.

CARPÉ ROSÉ: Seizing the opportunité to drink rosé.

HUMP DÉ: When a glass of rosé, or two, is enjoyed on Wednesday to get over the midweek hump.

INFINITÉ: The unquantifiable amount of love that exists in the universe for rosé.

NAMASTÉ: A greeting or gesture among friends before yoga class to indicate that, after Shavasana, you will be grabbing a glass.

PROVENCE, BROOKLYN: The hometown of Yes Way Rosé. We may not have been born in the South of France, but we sure were in spirit. Can be adopted to your rosé drinking location, for example, Provence, Chicago.

PSÉ: A public service announcement of breaking rosé news.

ROSÉ CHIC: Anything stylish and rosé pink. For example: The to-die-for Christian Dior gown Jennifer Lawrence tripped over when she won her Oscar in 2013 was rosé chic.

ROSÉ FRITES: A delicious, French-inspired pairing of rosé and fries, steak optional.

ROSÉ LIT: A written work (i.e., this book) that either inspires pouring a glass of rosé, drops knowledge about the subject, or simply has a pink cover.

Ketchup

ROSÉ PONG: An elevated collegiate game to play—in moderation—using delicious rosé in lieu of traditional beer. Use clear plastic cups for a most Insta-worthy occasion.

ROSÉ VIBES: A term that represents the all-encompassing positive spirit of rosé.

ROSÉ VIDA: Costa Ricans have it right with their outlook on *Pura Vida,* meaning "pure life," and their simple, relaxed way of being. Add rosé to the equation and you have Rosé Vida. *See also:* drinking rosé while vacationing in Costa Rica.

ROSÉVORE: Someone whose alcoholic beverage diet is limited to rosé and rosé only.

R&R&R: A state of rest, relaxation, and rosé.

SELFÉ: A FOMO-inducing photograph with rosé as the main attraction that usually generates a large number of "likes."

Acknowledgments

We are profoundly grateful for all of the love and support that helped us create this book, and everything Yes Way Rosé, while we're at it!

Shout Out To:

The entire team at Running Press, especially our superb editor Shannon Fabricant for the encouragement and guidance, as well as Frances Soo Ping Chow, Michael Clark, Christina Palaia, and Amanda Richmond.

Our literaré agent Alison Fargis for believing in the vision from the start.

The brilliant creative team who gave this book their all and made it a wildly special experience. Sara Kerens, our all-time favorite photographer and travel buddy, your incredible talent and patience know no bounds. Thank you for capturing YWR so perfectly (and also for fixing our hair and telling us when we look dead in the eyes). Maria del Mar Cuadra, a true collaborator and visionairé, we couldn't have done this without your hard work, delicious recipes, and meticulous styling. We wish you could make us lunch every day. Prop master extraordinaire Chelsea Maruskin, your passion and style shine in these photos. Whitney Pollett, for giving this book your magical touch and dreamy illustrations. Veronica Spera, for the many tasty contributions. And Iris Terrisson, the coolest intern ever, for helping in any way possible (even when it required turning on your French attitude).

Meg McNeill, our rosé soul mate and go-to expert, for sharing your beautiful voice. You inspire us dailé with your humor and total wine boss-ness.

Our ingenious contributors: Whitney Adams, Diane Corcoran, Natasha David, Jason Eisner, Kelly Hanifl, Julia Jaksic, Krystal Mack, Christine

Wright, Ashley Santoro, Stacey Swenson, and Stephanie Tadd. Special thanks to the lovely Agatha Kulaga and Erin Patinkin from Ovenly for creating our dream cake and Jordan Salcito for the kindness.

The many wonderful friends we've made in the biz who graciously offered their knowledge, contacts, and vineyards: Ariel Arce, Ryan Arnold, Ashwin Deshmukh, Nick Fauchald, Mikey Giugni, Colu Henry, Gina Hildebrand, Andrew Jones, Melinda Kearney and Michele Ouellet, Jean Francois Ott, Lily Peachin, our bro Josh Rosenstein, and Harry (Yes) Waye.

Cardi B for releasing *Invasion of Privacy*(é) while we wrote this book and needed it most.

The Yes Way Familé, who bring the dream world to life:

Denise DeBaun, our not-so-secret weapon, for helping us to find our way and being our trustworthy adviser on this wild ride. Everyone at Prestige and Johnson Brothers for the passion and support. It means the world to us. Chris Marino for always having our back. Karen Steinberg for the sanité (lol). Our publicist Leah Herman for the fabulous ideas and keeping it real. Susan Magsamen for talking to us at all hours, regardless of where you are in the world. And Max Stein for helping us get this (yes way) under way.

Our dear friends for reliably being there to lend a hand and clever caption. Thank you for learning not to touch your food or wine until we get the shot. But just because we've finished the book doesn't mean the rules change. :) We love you and we did this together.

From EB: I am very grateful for my rosé-converted family, who are now usually decked in Yes Way. Thank you to my number one editor, Mom, and my sisters Julie, Becca, and Melanie for the unconditional love. Thank you, Alex, Jeremy, Scott, and all of my minis—Lilly, Paisley, Isaac, Miles, Elias, and Oscar—for making me the happiest Auntie. Lots of love to my

Bubbe and extended fam. All of you motivate me to make the world a more rosé place.

From NH: Thank you to my awesome family for supporting me along my journé. Mom and Lee, Daddy daddy daddy and Susan, I couldn't have done it without you. Thank you for always believing in me, even when you kinda didn't, but then we proved you wrong. :) I love you all very much! To my number one Bro Adam for taking unflattering pictures of me and making me laugh. To Sam, Ben, Molly, Gabe, and Katie for making our family so much fun. And to my amazing godson, Colson: I can't wait to drink rosé with you one day! xo

Thank you to the following designers, brands, and wineries for their generosité: Becca PR, Bing Bang, Demetria Estates, Field Recordings, Gigi Burris, Madewell, Mociun, Moet + Chandon, Andrew Molleur, Nike Communications, Rebecca Taylor, Riedel, Sterling Vineyards, Underwest Donuts, Upstream Wine, Veda, WeWork South Williamsburg, Williamsburg Pizza, and Workshop Studio.

Lastlé, to every person who has followed us, tagged us on Instagram, shared a bottle of YWR with friends, and connected to our mission, we do this for you. We raise a glass to you, our Yes Way Communité, and to all the good times to come.

Index

D

E

F

N

O

P